SYNERGY:
Music and the
Liberal Arts

Robert L. Martin

Robert L. Martin
P. O. Box 1045
Kimberton, Pennsylvania 19442
www.snrg.info

Book Layout © 2017 BookDesignTemplates.com

Synergy: Music and the Liberal Arts/ Robert L Martin. -- 1st ed.
ISBN 978-0-578-31486-0

For Katherine Gould-Martin
and
Lihua Ying

CONTENTS

CHAPTER ONE

Introduction: A Career Built on Two Educations

In 2002 I had the idea of starting a new conservatory of music as part of the college where I was working, Bard College in Annandale-on-Hudson, New York. The circumstances were right: the College had just built a fine new performing arts center designed by the famous architect Frank Gehry; there was a mood of excitement and optimism at the College; the president of the College, Leon Botstein, was (and is) an orchestra conductor as well as college president, and he welcomed and encouraged big ideas. He liked the idea of starting a conservatory, so long as it was interestingly different from existing conservatories. I had an idea for how our conservatory could be distinctive, based on my early experiences as an undergraduate student.

Within twenty-four months the new Bard Conservatory was approved by the trustees of the College; fifteen months after that, in August, 2005, it opened its doors to its first cohort of twenty-one students. Fourteen years later, in June, 2019, I stepped down as director and now, two years after that, I offer this small book in the spirit of reflection on what was, for me, an enormously exciting adventure.

I had been extremely fortunate to be able to combine music study in a fine conservatory with an undergraduate education in an equally fine liberal arts college. It was not easy to accomplish, largely because the two schools were entirely separate and the arrangement was unprecedented. My experience made the idea of creating a conservatory within Bard College very attractive. Also, over the decades in which I pursued a career both in music and in the field of philosophy, I spoke often with musically and intellectually talented young people who faced pressure to decide between conservatory and college, while they wanted both. I was excited by the idea that we could create a place for such students.

There were already in the United States at least two conservatories within liberal arts colleges, the Oberlin Conservatory in Oberlin, Ohio, and the Lawrence Conservatory in Appleton, Wisconsin. Although these conservatories are within these colleges, the students can study only music, without completing a college degree, which is in fact what most tend to do. The distinguishing idea of the Bard Conservatory was that the double degree would be required, not optional. The Bachelor of Music degree would be awarded with the Bachelor of Arts degree in a field other than music, or not at all. Every undergraduate student in the Bard Conservatory would be a double-degree student. To explain my thinking about this, I need to say more about my own experience as a student.

Starting at the beginning (but briefly, I promise): I was born in 1940, in Philadelphia, Pennsylvania. My father was a union organizer and my mother was a high school English teacher. I grew up first in Portsmouth, Ohio, and later in Cincinnati, Ohio, where I began music lessons, first piano and then cello. I had the wonderful good fortune that Cincinnati was rich in music, and some of my junior high school musical friends (including violinist Linda Sharon Cerone and pianist James Levine) went on to distinguished careers in music. At the age of sixteen I attended the Meadowmount School of Music in upstate New York to study for the summer with the great cellist, Leonard Rose. He suggested that I come to the Curtis Institute in Philadelphia that fall, but a conversation with my parents led to the decision that I would return to Cincinnati to finish my junior year of high school and go to Curtis the following fall. At Meadowmount, I became friends with many Curtis students who provided me with a vivid picture of their daily lives during the school year, a picture that would prove important later.

Back in Cincinnati I attended a high school (Walnut Hills), modeled on the Boston Latin School, that was decidedly college preparatory. When it came time to make plans for the next year at Curtis, my high school advisor made the audacious suggestion that I try to start college at the same time, even though I would have finished only my junior year of high school. With his encouragement, I wrote to colleges in the Philadelphia area and heard from one of them, Haverford College (located outside of Philadelphia, approximately one hour distant from Curtis), that I could indeed be considered for admission. That spring I was accepted at both Curtis and Haverford College and spent the next months trying to convince Curtis to allow me to enroll at both (Haverford was already agreeable). I argued, with more self-assurance than was justified, that I could manage the workload; I was convinced that my Curtis friends stayed up very late most nights enjoying a variety of extra-curricular activities, which, if I would forego them, could be replaced by equivalent time for studies. Curtis finally agreed that I could proceed with the plan, on probation for the first semester, to see if would work.

As I look back on the months and years that followed, I am struck by two very different strands in my experiences along the double-degree path. One is the extraordinary encouragement and help I received from so many people. Teachers, friends, fellow students, college administrators, and many others applauded and rewarded my audaciousness. The other strand was the always repeated, or implied, question: when are you going to decide whether you really want to be a musician? This was most explicit from the administration of the Curtis Institute, but I felt it from my cello teacher and, in one form or another, from most of my Curtis classmates. I felt it most clearly, and most painfully, when, after five years at Curtis and two summers at the Marlboro Festival, I was told I could not return to Marlboro "because places are reserved for those who will pursue a career in music." A few months before receiving that letter, I had decided to accept an offer of a fellowship to begin graduate study in philosophy at Yale University instead of auditioning for a position in the cello section of a symphony orchestra.

I want to emphasize both of these strands in my experiences, one positive and one negative. On the one hand, I felt very fortunate and privileged to be able to pursue both music and other studies. Years later this contributed to my strong motivation, when the opportunity arose, to make the opportunity available to others. On the other hand, I often felt alone—in "no-mans-land", something of an odd duck, marginalized—and the result was my strong motivation, years later, to create a community of support for students like me.

These elements came together in the idea I had as to what would be different about the new conservatory at Bard. Because all undergraduate Conservatory students would pursue the double-degree program they would likely support each other. This would be important especially in those times when the workload would be intense, and the inevitable hesitations and self-doubts would arise. And the fact that the program was required, not optional, would be important in a different way for faculty. I knew that almost all the faculty would be conservatory-trained, and it would be natural for them therefore to lean toward an exclusive focus on music. The fact of the requirement meant that a faculty member needed to help the student navigate the program if the student was to remain in the program. This help—sometimes expressed just as a modicum of patience—would be critical to the student's success.

The years of double-degree study were happy ones for me. In the years after I finished my formal education I had wonderful career experiences, with joint music-philosophy appointments at several universities and also periods where one or the other was my primary activity. I always felt fortunate to have had the opportunities that my education provided, and this feeling made me even more eager to seize the chance, when it came, to create a conservatory that would offer similar possibilities to its students.

***

This book has three further chapters. The next is a piece I wrote in 2012 and have revised over the years, On the Education of Musicians: A Manifesto. It contains the core argument for my claim that young musicians need and deserve a first-class liberal arts education.

I wrote the paper as part of a plenary session at the annual meeting of the Association of European Conservatories of Music, held that year in St. Petersburg, Russia. In fact, Leon Botstein had been invited to speak but was unable to attend and recommended me in his place. The theme of the plenary session was integrity, and I struggled to find a way to connect that theme with what I actually wanted to speak about, which was of course our new conservatory. I hit on the idea of appealing to the sense of the word "integrity" that implies the wholeness and soundness of a structure, as when we say that weakened beams threaten the integrity of a house, or that a key part is integral to the workings of an engine. I wanted to make the case that a liberal arts education is, or should be, an integral part of a fine musical education. I was acutely aware, of course, that I would be speaking to a gathering of the heads of some of the finest institutions of music education in the world, and I would be arguing, in a way, that their institutions, focused on music alone, lacked integrity!

I worked hard on the paper, trying not only to respond to the usual objections (for example, that there is simply not enough time for a student to practice enough) but also to explain why, in my view, a liberal arts education will make one a better musician, not only a happier or a more successful musician. I thought about the history of the founding of the great conservatories of Europe, and that led me to the conviction that part of the story is one of social class and class prejudice. I wrote about nineteenth century Romantic conceptions of music and musicians, which seem curiously to have served as excuses for denying young musicians access to a first class education. I was relieved and gratified with the warm and positive response the paper received. In the days and even in the months and years after the presentation, directors of other conservatories expressed their agreement and said they wished they were able to implement, or at least experiment with, the kind of program we had begun at Bard. They said they were kept from doing so mainly by the traditions surrounding the conservatories and their partner universities, which drew a sharp line between "academic" studies and vocational training in the performing and fine arts.

Chapter Three is a brief history of the Bard Conservatory, with emphasis on the challenges faced and the critical decisions made. I wrote the main part of this history in 2015 in response to the many questions I was often asked: how were the faculty selected, how was the Conservatory funded, how did the integration with the College work, how did you deal with language difficulties? Later I added two short sections, one on the creation of the US-China Music Institute within the Bard Conservatory in 2018—one of the most exciting and important developments in the history of the Conservatory—and another on the exciting new leadership of the Conservatory: Dean Tan Dun and Director Frank Corliss. I hope this history provides the reader with a bridge from the ideas of the Manifesto to the practical realities of building an institution.

In Chapter Four we hear the voices of graduates of the Bard Conservatory, writing especially about their experiences navigating the double-degree. The students were the focus and heart, for me, of the experience of the Conservatory, and they are an extraordinary group! These are young people who took a chance on a new institution, choosing Bard in most cases over very attractive alternatives and pushing themselves to meet the challenges of our curriculum. Some students came to Bard already convinced that they wanted a broad educational experience. Others came despite the double-degree requirement: they were attracted by the extraordinary faculty and the strong financial aid. For some in this group, it took years before they saw the benefits of our curriculum; some even left, only to return after a year or so. It was especially gratifying and exciting to witness the personal transformations that took place as the magic of intellectual curiosity and learning took hold. In this section we have the reflections of many of these students, now with the perspective provided by the passing of years. Many now have careers in music, and others are working in the fields of their second majors. After all, it is the stories of these students that will tell us the most about the value of a liberal arts education for young people with extraordinary musical talent.

This book is a tree with many roots. For the chance to develop the Manifesto I owe thanks to Leon Botstein's thoughtful idea of suggesting me as his replacement as plenary speaker at the Association of European Conservatories of Music. For the push to write a history of the Bard Conservatory, I thank Ann Gabler, Frank Corliss, and others who thought it was time, after ten years into the life of the Conservatory, and before facts became myths, to tell the story of its creation and first years. For the idea of a document in Chinese, I owe thanks to Jingyu Mao, former student and good friend, who pointed out that the name of the Bard Conservatory was well known in the music world of China but not the double-degree idea behind it. I offer special thanks to Yichun Wu, a graduate of the Bard Conservatory, who not only translated most of the material of this book but also assisted me throughout the process. I thank Katherine Gould-Martin for problem solving sessions during our two years of morning walks around the Lietzensee in Berlin, and our son Benjamin for expert proof reading. Special thanks to Lihua Ying, my advisor in all things.

Chapter Two

On the Education of Musicians: a Manifesto[1]

Aristotle wrote that young people would profit from the study of music but should give it up well before the point of becoming professionals. He agreed with Plato that music brings harmony to the souls of the young, but he drew a clear line between well-bred gentlemen and professional musicians.

> "The right measure will be obtained if students of music stop short of the arts which are

---

[1] An early version of this essay was presented in a panel, "Aspects of the Notion of Artistic Integrity" at the 2012 Annual Congress of the Association Européenne des Conservatoires, Académies de Musique et Musikhochschulen, 10 Nov 2012. A revised version, which owes much to the helpful comments of George Rose, appeared in The Place of Music: Essays from the first decade of the Bard College Conservatory of Music (2016). The current version contains further revisions.

> practiced in professional contests...for in this the performer practices the art, not for the sake of his own improvement, but in order to give pleasure, and that of a vulgar sort, to his hearers. For this reason, the execution of such music is not the part of a freeman but of a paid performer..."[2]

This is an early example of a long-lasting class prejudice. Musicians, actors, jugglers, comics, and other entertainers have been treated throughout history essentially as servants, not as fellow citizens. Joseph Haydn is a prime example, responsible not only for composing and performing for the prince and his guests, but also for the laundry of the court musicians. A first-class education, historically, was deemed appropriate for those who would assume leadership positions in society, not for the working classes and not for the entertainers (and incidentally, not for women, although that gradually changed). It is striking that the founding of the first great modern conservatory in the western world, that of Paris in 1795, was a socially progressive, forward-looking attempt to bring dignity to the profession. It was felt that those who would play in the theaters and concert halls should be not only adept at the instrument but also grounded in aural skills, solfeggio, and music history. This was a big step forward from the time of the founding of the first conservatories in the West, in

---

[2] Aristotle's *Politics*: Translated by Benjamin Jowett 8-6.

the fourteenth century, when orphans in the Italian *ospedali* were trained to play and sing in public to solicit charity for their food and lodging. But the education received at the Paris Conservatory in no way matched that received by the children of the upper classes, because it was restricted almost entirely to music. Amazingly little has changed since then. Randall Thompson put it quite simply in 1967:

> "The direction of a conservatory is frankly vocational. That of a Liberal Arts College is not. The aim of a Liberal Arts college is to produce integrated citizens. "[3]

I think it is time to realize that young musicians not only need, but also deserve, a first-class education in the liberal arts and sciences.

It is tempting to come to a very different conclusion. The length and intensity of training needed for a career as a professional musician exceeds that of even the most well-known specialties, such as brain surgeon. So why should a budding musician waste time with a liberal arts education?[4] That is the first question I will try to answer here, by arguing that a liberal arts education is not only

---

[3] College Music: An Investigation for the Association of American Colleges (New York, 1935), p. 97.

[4] From now on I will use the phrase "liberal arts" in the broad sense, to include the sciences as well as the humanities and social sciences.

valuable but also crucial in the education of young musicians. After that I will try to answer a second question: where does the idea come from that gifted young musicians should focus exclusively, or almost exclusively, on music?

My argument for the necessity, not just the desirability, of a liberal arts education has three parts. The first two parts present important though not ultimately decisive considerations in support of this claim, but the third part presents a consideration that I think is indeed decisive.

1. **Other things being equal, the life of a musician with a solid general education will be richer and happier than that of one without it.**

I suppose this is hardly controversial, yet it is important nonetheless. All the parts of a liberal arts education—the single courses taken as part of the exploratory phase of one's education, or the in-depth study that constitutes a "major"—will in later years become sources of pleasure and edification. Not coincidentally, the broad education will connect one to other interesting people at many stages of one's life. Even for a busy, successful performing artist there will be vacations, sabbaticals, and perhaps even retirement, all of which will be enriched by knowledge of other subjects and possession of the skills for exploring them. If later life should bring the need for a career change—a possibility that looms large for any musician, however unwelcome it may be—there is no question but that a liberal arts education will be of great service in pointing the way to options.

2. **A liberal arts education provides a career advantage in music.**

The ease and self-confidence in writing and speaking that comes from a liberal arts education helps a musician in a wide variety of practical ways, from pre-concert talks and the preparation of program materials to negotiations with employers and funders. Further, one need only think of Yo-Yo Ma's Silk Road project, for example, to see the power of a career-enhancing idea born of knowledge of history and the imagination to ask penetrating questions. This is a point of broad applicability. The day of the narrowly focused performing career is for the most part over. We see entrepreneurial projects of all kinds, often but not always involving technology, that are initiated by young musicians, and these require multiple skills. For many, the move into some aspect of arts management flows naturally from their backgrounds as professional musicians and may even develop alongside their activities as performers; this requires an extension of their skill sets and habits of mind, to which a liberal arts education will bring an immeasurable advantage.

3. **A liberal arts education will make a musician a better musician, adding refinement, discrimination, and imagination to technical prowess.**

This is the part of the argument most in need of justification. Points (1) and (2) are important but not decisive. One could grant that a liberal arts education brings pleasure and career advantages and offers alternatives, yet argue that, when it comes to the music itself, it is the years of practice, study with master teachers, and performance experience, on top of the essential ingredient of musical talent, that determines the quality of the outcome and that may even require not pursuing a broad education. Indeed, some would argue that it is the willingness to sacrifice a great deal—including the personal and career advantages of a liberal arts education—that characterizes the most dedicated musicians, that allows them, through single-minded focus, to become great musicians. I think this is wrong, and I will try to show it is wrong. I will argue that the skills and attitudes fostered by an education in the liberal arts and sciences are exactly those that will make the difference between technical excellence and genuine artistry.

What kind of argument is possible here? I assume that the reader recognizes the difference be-tween technical excellence and genuine artistry. We have all heard performances that are frustrating because they are, in a sense, faultless, but still unaffecting and uninteresting. The performance may be well in tune and rhythmically solid, with pleasing sound and generally "musical" phrasing, good tempo and ample energy. There are no "mistakes", yet our minds wander. By contrast, a performance of authentic artistry holds our attention. We recognize a palpable sense of concentration and of overall direction among the parts of the piece, either forward toward what is coming or reflective of what has been heard; there is a sense of freshness and discovery, as though the performer is in-venting the piece; there is moment-to-moment characterization of musical materials, expressive of wit, drama, pathos, longing, grandeur, and mystery; and there is even more – all quite difficult to characterize in words but conspicuous in performance.

Who is to say where artistry comes from? We speak of musical talent, and anyone who has worked with young musicians for many years knows how important but also elusive that concept is. I have argued elsewhere that at least part of musical talent is responsiveness to the "stuff" of music: rhythms, chord progressions, textures, timbres, silences, and the other things out of which musical works are constructed.[5] But talent alone does not produce artistry. Artistry is

[5] R. Martin, "Musical 'Topics' and Expression in Music," *Journal of Aesthetics and Art Criticism* volume 54 number 4 (1995).

exquisitely sensitive to the details of particular works. The qualities strengthened by a liberal arts education include those that conduce toward the grasp of such details, and therefore toward artistry. These are the qualities of curiosity, intellectual adventurousness, the ability to see connections, and the mental discipline to focus on complex arguments and narratives. The day may come when we know enough about the human brain to quantify these neurological connections: how the study of mathematics can affect the performance of a Schubert piano sonata, or how the study of a foreign language and culture can affect the performance of a Bach suite. But even now we can recognize the result and know that it is real.

Let me give a more specific example of the ways that a liberal arts education can improve one's music making. There is an interesting musicological literature on the presence of "topics"—the Greek topoi—especially in music of the eighteenth century.[6] The topics are such things as the hunt, the church, the courtly dance, the forest, the village wedding. Musical references to these topics are present even in so-called "absolute" music: for example, a fragment of a horn call representing the hunt, or a modal chord progression representing church worship. These allusions were and remain recognizable (almost

---

[6] See, for example, W. J. Allanbrook, Rhythmic Gesture in Mozart (University of Chicago Press, 1983) and references included there.

unconsciously) as such by audiences, providing an extra-musical dimension. The result for the listener is a general sense of connection to the concerns of everyday life. What is the significance for the performer? To some extent the performer needs to "bring out" the topics; more importantly, a broadly educated performer will likely have background knowledge of the cultural phenomena represented by the topics. This, at the very least, will likely enhance the perform-er's concentration. It will communicate itself to the audience as a kind of insight and a source of delight.

One can imagine a number of objections to my claims about the value of a liberal arts education for music-making. One objection—surely the one most frequently made—is that there is simply not enough time for academic studies beyond the demands of the instrument. My experience is that gifted young people generally have more energy than they know what to do with, and that fewer hours of intelligent practice are much better than many hours of mindless practice. Furthermore, the level of technical accomplishment of young players has risen dramatically over the years. It is evident that many students arrive at conservatory needing musical refinement (and all that supports it) far more than hours of technical work.

In truth, having presented these arguments over the years, I have often been surprised by how readily these conclusions are accepted by my fellow musicians and music educators. That leads to the second question: where, then, does the idea come from that gifted young musicians should focus exclusively, or almost exclusively, on music? If this view is as misguided as I claim, what accounts for its stubborn hold?

I think there are two main factors at work here. The first, which I have already mentioned, I will call the Aristotle prejudice. It is the view, quite simply, that the kind of general education offered to the elite is not necessary or appropriate for the training of entertainers. That view, unfortunately, is alive and well today. Indeed, it is so familiar and ingrained that it is often difficult to recognize. It is reflected obliquely in the practice, in many countries, of placing young musicians and young athletes in special schools where they are trained rigorously in the hope that they will win international competitions. It is reflected also, more generally, in the fact that "Great Books" seminars are found mostly in small, expensive, private liberal arts colleges and less often in large public universities.

Another factor that contributes to the prevalent view of conservatory education is the nineteenth-century Romantic view of the musician as an exalted genius, a person of inspiration, madness, and obsessive focus, a person with a higher calling, in direct touch with a spiritual force. We all recognize this as a central conceit of Romantic literature, poetry and painting. A famous example is the persona of Beethoven that was constructed in the second half of the nineteenth century. We recognize this notion in the mystique surrounding Franz Liszt and other virtuosi at whose performances audience members were said to faint from excitement. We recognize the philosophical underpinnings of this notion in Schopenhauer's view that music—and only music—provides access to the Will, the world of things in themselves, otherwise entirely hidden from human view. The Romantic conception of musical genius, still very much alive today, teams up with the Aristotle prejudice: it makes peace with what I regard as the shortchanging of the young musician by glorifying single-mindedness. This is a potent and insidious combination: gifted musicians are denied access to the education associated with upper class opportunity, while being assured that the loss is not significant. The Romantic conception makes a virtue of an intellectual deficit!

Now of course there is much of value in the Romantic conception. The Romantics understood that music is not only pleasing but also deep; not only attractive but also revelatory. There is truth in the feeling that high musical attainment is wondrous, even magical. But there is nothing in Romanticism that should keep a young musician of the highest aspirations from having a fine general education. One can hold that high musical talent is extraordinary and mysterious, and still advocate for the benefits of broad knowledge. One can be inspired and in touch with the muses and still profit from a rigorous liberal arts education. The artistry is enhanced by the education.

Where do these conclusions lead? In my view, they show the need for a fundamental change of culture, something on a par with the bold idea that led to the creation of the Paris Conservatory. The idea then was to elevate music from the street to the dignity of serious study. The next step is long overdue: to elevate the education of musicians to the finest that society has to offer. The current culture is perpetuated by the private instrumental teachers in the conservatories who, are, with few exceptions, trained in conservatories and who therefore share the dominant viewpoint of the conservatories: that their students should focus exclusively, or almost exclusively, on music. Besides constituting the leadership of most conservatories, the private instrumental teachers have the strongest influence on their students' attitudes, often beginning when the students are very young. We need to create a new system with opportunities that make a liberal arts education possible for gifted young musicians without sacrificing their musical education, and that includes arrangements and incentives that make this possibility attractive for all concerned. As guiding principles for change, I suggest:

1.Young musicians should have access to a fine liberal arts education within existing comprehensive academic institutions, as it is provided to their peers, not specially packaged and im-ported into the conservatory. That is, musicians should be in classes along with those studying subjects other than music and who are preparing for all kinds of careers and professions.

2.The natural and mathematical sciences, and social sciences, should be included in the liberal arts curriculum, not only the humanities. A basic understanding of science and evidence is necessary for every citizen in today's world.

3.Musical and liberal arts studies should be flexibly integrated, allowing students a wide variety of ways to combine the two over a reasonably long period of years. (This will require flexibility on both sides.)

4.Mentoring should be provided, recognizing that double degree studies are demanding and of-ten frustrating.

It may perhaps be clear and not surprising that my conception of a liberal arts education is that of the American liberal arts college or university. The key feature of this conception, and where it differs most significantly from post-secondary education in most of the rest of the world, is that it is seen as preparation, not specialization. Students typically have up to two years before choosing a major, and even the major is usually seen as preparing the student for specialized graduate or professional study which comes later. This idea is, relatively speaking, a late departure from the system of the German universities from which so many features of the American university system are derived. Only in 1901 did the Harvard Medical School, for example, require a bachelor's degree for admission; before that most students began medical and other professional studies immediately after secondary school, as they still do in most of the rest of the world. The idea of "liberalization before professionalization" may well have been "the most important reform in the history of American higher education."[7] The university in Berlin, according to the design of Wilhelm von Humboldt in the early years of the nineteenth century, was to promote the acquisition of new knowledge, taking for granted that the secondary schools would "effectively feed into the higher academic institutions." The purpose of the schools, Humboldt wrote, was to "prepare the mind for pure scholarship"[8]: to produce young men who had already achieved a broad general education and were ready to work

---

[7] The Rise of the Research University: A Sourcebook, edited by L. Menand, P. Reitter, and C. Wellmon (2017) p. 229.

[8] "On the Internal Structure of the University in Berlin and Its Relationship to other Organizations" (1809) by Wilhelm von Humboldt, translated and included in The Rise of the Research University: A Sourcebook, p.112.

alongside their professors in specialized subjects. The gymnasia of mid-nineteenth-century Berlin to which Humboldt referred were attended by a tiny minority of privileged males, and their preparation was no doubt excellent. Whether Humboldt's expectations were realistic, and whether they are reasonable today, it was the view of educators in mid-nineteenth-century America, as well as today, that young people needed far more in the way of general education than what they received in secondary schools. Many American educators also felt that undergraduates were too young to make wise decisions about what field to pursue.[9] For this combination of reasons, the conception of the liberal arts college as preparation took root in American higher education. It is this conception that I have particularly in mind as that which young musicians both need and deserve, though versions of it can of course be obtained within the context of other educational systems.

We attempted to create a prototype of such a new system at the Bard Conservatory, founded in 2005. The fundamental idea was that all Conservatory students will pursue two degrees simultaneously, over a five-year period: the Bachelor of Music degree and the Bachelor of Arts degree in a field other than

---

[9] See, for example, the comments of Noah Porter in his 1871 Inaugural Address as president of Yale University, reprinted in The Rise of the Research University: A Sourcebook, p.258.

music. The double degree is required, not optional; it is understood that the student can continue at the Bard Conservatory only within the double degree program. The high success rate of our graduates in gaining admission to the most competitive graduate programs in the U.S. and abroad has been heartening. More than 90 percent continue in music; some choose to pursue graduate or professional study in other fields. I describe the early history of the Bard College Conservatory of Music in Chapter Three.

A Brief History of the Bard College Conservatory of Music[10]

O n the evening of Tuesday, May 7, 2002, I hurried from Penn Station, having just arrived from Baltimore, to Riverside Church on the Upper West Side of Manhattan to attend the gala dinner of Bard's Center for Curatorial Studies. In Baltimore I had interviewed for the position of dean of the Peabody Conservatory of Music. I was a candidate for the position because I was intrigued by the idea of leading a school of music, especially one connected to a fine university—in this case, Johns Hopkins University. By the time I was on the train

---

[10] I wrote this in 2015 to celebrate the tenth birthday of the Bard Conservatory. It is updated in a few places, especially at the end.

back to New York I had decided to withdraw my candidacy, and I was excited by a new idea: why not start a Conservatory as part of Bard College? I arrived at the gala dinner in time for the cocktail hour and found myself alone in conversation with Bard President Leon Botstein. I mentioned to President Botstein that I had briefly considered being a candidate for the deanship at Peabody, but now wondered how he would feel about the idea of creating our own Conservatory at Bard. He replied at once that it was a good idea, and that I should take some time to visit other conservatories to see how we could create something truly distinctive. The decision to move ahead toward a Bard Conservatory of Music was taken that evening around 7 p.m. I look back on that evening, and on the months and years that followed, with undiminished amazement at the boldness of Leon Botstein in agreeing to create a conservatory, and deep gratitude for his strong support throughout.

Figure 1 Leon Botstein, President of Bard College

Figure 2 The Bard Conservatory Orchestra in Berlin's Konzerthaus

It was no coincidence that I was attracted to the idea of the combination of a music conservatory and a college or university. I had attended the Curtis Institute of Music and Haverford College together over a five-year period, earning a bachelor of music degree in cello performance and a bachelor of arts degree in philosophy. It had been a wonderful experience for me, but it could have been improved by coordination between the two institutions, or better yet, by the existence of the two programs within one institution. Bard seemed perfect not only because its president is a world-class musician and because it was just completing construction of a major performance venue—the Richard B. Fisher Center for the Performing Arts—but also because Bard has a history of bold and innovative educational initiatives.

Two years later, on May 21, 2004, a formal proposal was approved by the trustees of the College: "The proposal is to create a small conservatory on the Bard College campus—known as the Conservatory at Bard College—in which all students pursue not only the traditional conservatory degree (bachelor of music) but also the bachelor of arts degree in a field other than music. Such a program, in which no separate bachelor of music degree is offered, would be unique in the United States today."

In the two years between the birth of the idea and the approval of its creation, there were four particularly crucial ingredients: research on other Conservatories, the participation of Melvin Chen, the recruiting of faculty, and the shaping of a distinctive curriculum.

I traveled to Oberlin in the summer of 2002 and met with its director of admission, Michael Mandaren, and several of its faculty. The Oberlin Conservatory was founded in 1867, only two years after the founding of the distinguished liberal arts college, and the two have been fully unified ever since.

The Oberlin Conservatory is noted for the fact that its students may pursue a five-year, double-degree program toward the Conservatory degree and the Oberlin College B.A. degree. It was therefore the obvious model for our program. Mandaren was gracious and helpful in answering my questions. I learned that Oberlin's double-degree program is its signature program: approximately 70% of all applicants express interest in pursuing it. I also learned that, generally speaking, the liberal arts faculty are very favorable toward the idea of admitting Conservatory double-degree applicants. By contrast, Conservatory faculty are generally less enthusiastic about the applicants who plan to pursue the double-degree option. Given the choice between two applicants of approximately equal musical ability, the Conservatory faculty member is likely to prefer the one who wishes to study only at the Conservatory. The reason given is that the former student is likely to be "distracted" from the study of music, and/or to decide to pursue a non-music career, in which case the investment will not have paid off. Tellingly, only about 15% of students graduating from the Conservatory complete the double-degree program, even though a far higher percentage begin in it. Faculty seem to regard the double degree as very difficult and definitely not suitable for most students; I learned this from my own conversations with Oberlin faculty whom I've known for many years.

I also visited the Shepherd School of Music of Rice University, and studied the programs of the other school noted for its five-year double-degree program, Lawrence University in Appleton, Wisconsin, as well as those of the New England Conservatory, the Eastman School of Music, The Juilliard School, and the schools of music associated with large universities such as the University of Michigan, Indiana University, and the University of Southern California. I arrived at two conclusions: (1) that double-degree students in all of these schools tend to feel marginal and isolated, and (2) that bias against the double-degree program is part of the culture of these institutions, at least in part because most of the faculty are graduates of traditional conservatory programs that focus only on music.

My conclusion, therefore, was that the Bard Conservatory should adopt the policy that the double-degree program be required, not optional. Our students would thereby not be marginal, and indeed might be likely to support and help each other. New students would learn from the experiences of more advanced students. Furthermore, faculty, having agreed to teach at the Bard Conservatory and knowing our policy, would be likely to resist the inclination to counsel students toward an exclusive focus on music studies.

Melvin Chen joined the Bard faculty in the fall of 2001, teaching both in the Music Program and in a variety of programs in the Division of Science, Mathematics, and Computing. I first met him when he performed in the 2000 Bard Music Festival. I was impressed by his performances and by his education: B.S. from Yale in physics and chemistry, M.M. from Juilliard in piano and violin, Ph.D. in chemistry from Harvard. Melvin and I became good friends. From the time that the idea of the Bard Conservatory was born, we talked endlessly about every aspect of how it might work. He was an obvious "poster child" for the guiding double-degree idea. In February 2004, when Melvin was in his third year of teaching at Bard and as I was preparing the proposal to Bard's Board of Trustees to launch the Conservatory, I invited Melvin to become associate director of the Conservatory, a position he held until he left to become professor of piano and deputy dean of the Yale School of Music in 2012.

Figure 3 Melvin Chen

Melvin had a very strong influence on the shaping of the Bard Conservatory, for at least the following three reasons. First, he was very good at seeing the implications of seemingly small decisions that we needed to make—seeing the precedents that would be set and the difficulties that might arise from various choices. It was extremely helpful to have someone so quick, so knowledgeable, and so strategically-minded to discuss things with. Second, he had a very clear sense of how prospective and current students would react to policy decisions we might make, partly, I suppose, because he was fairly close in age to those students. Third, he had a range of contacts in the music world quite different from mine, again because of age; it helped that he was liked and admired by all who knew him. This was of enormous help in recruiting faculty and finding strategies for recruiting students. Beyond these three qualities, however, it was simply the extremely high level of Melvin's achievement and the high standards to which he held himself that made the most difference to the life of the Conservatory.

The recruiting of an extraordinary faculty was perhaps the most important factor in the early and continued success of the Conservatory. Before starting the process I traveled to Philadelphia for a very helpful, detailed conversation with Robert Fitzpatrick, then dean at Curtis. He filled me in on the details of their audition process, on the financial arrangements with faculty, on support for students traveling to New York City for lessons, on arrangements for orchestra and chamber music, and on many other matters. It was that meeting that led me to see that the roster system for faculty—paid by the hour for lessons actually given—would serve us well, just as it did Curtis. It was important to learn that the Manhattan School and Mannes College, both in New York City, also operated on the roster system, and that it seemed to suit busy artists whose availability and priorities were liable to change frequently. I spoke first with pianist Richard Goode, whom I knew from our years of study together, first at Marlboro and then at the Curtis Institute. Richard did not, and still does not, teach on a regular basis at any school, but he agreed to join our roster to give master classes on a regular basis. His agreement, even on that limited basis, was very helpful in further recruiting. His willingness to let his name be used on Bard's roster had a positive effect on others I invited.

Figure 4 Melvin Chen, Richard Goode, Robert Martin

Then followed meetings with many wonderful musicians, some of whom I knew from Curtis (Arnold Steinhardt and Michael Tree from the Guarneri

Quartet, the pianist Peter Serkin) and others from various previous encounters in the music world (violinist Laurie Smukler and violist Ira Weller, violinists Ida and Ani Kavafian, cellist Peter Wiley, and many others). In every case I offered several features that seemed attractive: that they would teach only students whom they wished to teach, that if their schedule did not permit trips to Bard, we would send the student to New York City for lessons, and that when they did come to Bard to teach we would supplement their schedules with chamber music coaching, paid at the same hourly rate as the individual lessons. Above all, I promised that the students would be interesting, intelligent, and highly motivated. Some asked why the double degree was mandatory instead of optional; my answer (explained above) seemed to satisfy them, and I had an almost 100% success rate in recruiting the faculty we wanted.

Melvin Chen was very helpful in faculty recruiting. He knew, far better than I, the musicians of his generation, and he was able to steer me to many superb players and teachers whom I wouldn't have known otherwise (for example, flutist Tara Helen O'Connor). Another good source of faculty was the American Symphony. Clarinetist Laura Flax, trumpeter Carl Albach, and French hornist Jeffrey Lang came through that route.

We didn't advertise faculty openings, partly because we were not seeking to fill college positions in the usual sense but trying to find artist-teachers of a very special kind for the roster. We had a very clear sense of what we were looking for in these teachers. We asked ourselves who, among those who were based in New York City or relatively near Bard, and whose artistry we admired, would attract students of the highest level? We understood that most gifted and advanced young players, and their parents, know the teachers at the various conservatories and have dreams and preferences as to whom they would like to study with. It is no accident that many teachers we recruited also teach at Curtis or Juilliard. Where we were less familiar with the scene, as for example in the case of French horn, we inquired broadly of young professionals, "Who is the most distinguished horn teacher in the United States?" Then I arranged visits with these people and was, very fortunately, able to recruit them to join our roster.

It was clear to us early on that China would be an important area for student recruiting. The other top conservatories all had large numbers of string and piano students from China, very gifted and ambitious and eager to come to the United States. This presented us with an immediate problem: how would these students fare with the double-degree program, given the fact that in many cases their English language skills were weak? Would they even consider a program such as ours, given the fact that the top music high schools in China were famous for encouraging students to focus on music to the almost complete exclusion of their other studies? To help us answer these questions we turned to our friend, the violinist Weigang Li, founding first violinist of the Shanghai String Quartet. Weigang had attended the famous middle school attached to the Shanghai Conservatory and had maintained close connections throughout China since coming to the West. After hearing our plans and learning of our faculty, Weigang gave us his opinion: there would indeed be excellent students in China who, if offered the chance to study with the teachers on our roster, with very attractive financial aid, and with the understanding that they would also have to pursue the B.A. degree with a second major, would indeed come to Bard. He noted that many parents would be astonished and delighted that their children would have the opportunity to get a broad education, and that, generally speaking, the level of discipline and hard work of these students was high enough that our program would be possible for them. It was clear, of course, that we would need to offer intensive instruction in English as a Second Language if we wanted to recruit these students at the point at which they were ready to go abroad.

Weigang Li's opinion turned out to be correct. It was also greatly to our advantage that he agreed to join our faculty roster from the beginning. Not only did he attract students from China (and elsewhere), but he spoke directly with prospects and their families to explain our program, to give assurances, and, in many cases, to get information about the student's motivation that helped us make admission decisions. After the first year or so he was joined on our roster by another member of the Shanghai Quartet, Yiwen Jiang, who had studied and maintained contacts at the music high school attached to the Central Conservatory of Music in Beijing, and who helped us in similar ways.

While recruiting faculty we also worked at constructing the curriculum of the Conservatory. We had received a planning grant of $50,000 from the Mellon Foundation, and I used part of that to retain the composer Edward Harsh to study the curriculum and requirements of a wide array of conservatories and schools of music in the United States and to provide us with an analysis of the range of decisions to be made. His work, and our own discussions, including those with Leon Botstein, led to a number of important decisions about our curriculum. One was that the teaching of music theory needed to be changed significantly so that it was relevant to the actual performance of music. Another was that music theory should be integrated with relevant parts of music history. We also decided early on that every student in the Conservatory would have a least one semester of composition, as a capstone to the theory sequence and with the aim of deepening the performers' understanding of the process resulting in the composition of musical works. We decided also on an emphasis on chamber music.

The next step was the preparation of materials for publicizing the Conservatory and recruiting students. This required that we settle on a mission statement for the Conservatory and many matters of fine-tuning the "message" that we wished to convey. The question was forced on us: whom exactly were we intending to train, and what outcomes did we seek? We agreed that we wanted to convey the importance of a broad education without in any way downplaying the importance of focused dedication to music. Melvin Chen wrote the following, which we decided to use as a kind of preamble to the mission statement:

> Music, like all art, engages the mind and the heart. It redefines boundaries and questions limits in order to make a meaningful statement about the human condition. The education of the mind is, therefore, as important as the education of the fingers. The greatest musicians not only have the technical mastery to communicate effectively, but also are deeply curious and equally adept at analytical and emotional modes of thought.

Our mission statement simply assumes the correctness of that view as to the importance of a liberal arts education: *The mission of The Bard*

College Conservatory of Music is to provide the best possible preparation for a person dedicated to a life immersed in the creation and performance of music.

Our recruiting materials sought to appeal to two very different audiences (and those in between): on the one hand, those who are strongly drawn to a conservatory-only model, for example Curtis and Juilliard, and who need to be convinced that Bard will provide what they are looking for *in addition* to a college education; on the other hand, those excellent players who are strongly drawn to fine and prestigious universities and colleges, and need to be convinced that Bard will provide what they are looking for *in addition* to conservatory training at the highest level.

I can say in retrospect that, because Melvin Chen and I were so enthusiastic about the double-degree concept and had so much enjoyed our own integrated studies as undergraduates, we may have underestimated the difficulty of recruiting to the Bard Conservatory. Another way to put the same point is that we overestimated the size of the pool for recruiting: those who played well enough to be admitted to the top conservatories and who also could be drawn to see the value of a liberal arts education. We put a lot of thought into framing our message to reach that relatively small group. Over the years I worked on many presentations trying to make the case for the double-degree program: that it would actually help the student become a better musician. In 2012, when I had the opportunity to address a plenary session of the Association of European Conservatories of Music, I consolidated those presentations into an essay that has evolved into my paper, "On the Education of Musicians: A Manifesto."

Once the new Conservatory was officially approved by the trustees of Bard College in May 2004 with a projected opening date of fall 2005, we set out to recruit the first group of students. That summer I visited many festivals and schools in the United States, and in late November and December of 2004 Chen and I traveled to Taiwan, South Korea, and China. In each place we visited leading arts high schools, offering master classes in some places, meeting with faculty and administrators, and hearing students whenever possible. The situation in each country was different. In Shanghai, for example, there was sensitivity about having us hold auditions at the Middle School attached to the Shanghai Conservatory, even though many teachers there were eager to help their students arrange to study abroad. As a result, we were invited to join the auditions for a summer program in Canada, and then to speak informally with students who seemed good candidates for Bard. Overall, as a result of our visits to Shanghai and Beijing, eight students from China were recruited to start Bard in fall 2005. The opening class consisted or 21 students: 10 from China, 8 from the United

States, and one each from Germany, Malaysia, and Canada. Our recruiting continued throughout the spring and even into the summer.

Figure 5 The first twenty students at the Bard Conservatory

Looking back, it is clear that certain patterns were already beginning to emerge. Two of our first students—oboist Rachel Steinhorn, from the Chicago area, and clarinetist Sam Israel, from New Jersey— were players of conservatory quality but headed in the direction of science. They were perhaps not sure of that direction as 18-year-olds, and they took their music studies very seriously. Sam became one of the Biology Program's top students and Rachel became one of the Psychology Program's top students. After five years of study and two degrees, Sam went on to a Ph.D. program in biochemistry at the University of

California, Berkeley; Rachel went on to the Washington University School of Medicine in St. Louis. Of the other 19 students in that group, almost all went on to graduate school in music. The group was held together by a spirit of adventure and the realization that they were part of something new and significant.

On one of the first evenings of the semester we held a pizza and chamber music party: all of the students, Melvin Chen. and I, and, as I remember, violinist Weigang Li, who was already known to the eight Chinese students. We collected stacks of music, some of it purchased just days before the start of the semester, moved tables and brought in stands and chairs into four or five rooms, and quickly organized ensembles: a Mendelssohn Octet, a Dvořák string quintet, an Ibert woodwind piece, and various piano trios. It was a fine ice-breaking and bonding experience and, in a peculiar way, an unrepeatable experience, for the simple reason that only in the first year of the Conservatory would *all* the students arrive, meet for the first time, and begin school together. In subsequent years we had only the new students for the first three weeks—generally too few for a real chamber music party—and they were eagerly awaiting the arrival of the returning older students. New patterns of bonding and socialization developed in those subsequent years, quite effective and interesting in themselves. But the memory of that first pizza and chamber music party is a very special one.

Figure 6 The first students at the home of the Martins

In these first days of the Conservatory, our entire administrative staff consisted of four: besides Melvin Chen and me, Eileen Brickner and Fu-chen Chan. Eileen had worked with me as administrative assistant for many years before the opening of the Conservatory, when I was dean of graduate studies, associate dean of the college, and later vice president for academic affairs. In 2005 Eileen added the

Conservatory to her portfolio of responsibilities with the title of executive assistant; in later years she became the Conservatory's dean of students, a position she continues to hold even as I write this, in July 2020.   Fu-chen Chan, a flutist and free-lance musician in New York City, joined us in the summer of 2005 just before the first students arrived.   Fu-chen's role began as scheduler of lessons but quickly expanded in every direction over the years; she became the Conservatory manager and, later, dean of administration.   Along the way, Fu-chen created our Preparatory Division and managed it for several years. Those were indeed amazing and memorable months as the four of us confronted the exciting reality of students arriving and the Conservatory becoming real before our eyes.

International students and English language proficiency

It was clear at once during the first year that English language proficiency would be a very large and continuing problem for the Conservatory. On the one hand, the eight students from China—violinists, violists, and pianists—were, as a group, the strongest players in the Conservatory. They, with some of the others, set a high standard that established the level of the Conservatory as nothing else could have done. Within weeks we had performances both within Bard and in outside engagements that amazed the audiences. On the other hand, it was difficult to imagine how most of these eight Chinese students would survive academically. Their writing, especially, was very weak. The story was always the same: the teachers at their music high schools in China—the two most famous, one attached to the Central Conservatory of Music in Beijing, the other to the Shanghai Conservatory of Music—told them to focus only on their music studies and to pay as little attention as possible to their other studies, including English. Once we got to know these students—their talent, achievement, and discipline, as well as their sense of humor, charm, and integrity—we couldn't imagine the Conservatory without them (and without more like them), but at the same time we knew we had a problem on our hands.

The first step had to do with College admissions. Bard's Admission Office had (and has) a liberal policy with respect to international students in general, deemphasizing the standardized Test of English as a Second Language (TOEFL) and looking at individual applicants on a case-by-case basis. Still, it was essential to Admission that applicants be able to succeed in the required First-Year Seminar, and it was clear that our Chinese applicants were not at this level. Mary Backlund, director of Admission, helpfully suggested that we make use of an "Exception Admit" status that had been developed in earlier years for cases of applicants who had strong potential but (remediable) deficiencies. Students who were admitted with "Exception Admit" status would be fully matriculated but would need to make up the deficiencies (in our case, in English language competence) by the end of their first year, proceeding thereafter as regular admits. Our Exception Admit students would postpone taking the First-Year Seminar until their second year. During the first year we would provide them with an English as a Second Language (ESL) course.

All first-year Bard students arrive three weeks before the returning students to take the three-week Workshop in Language and Thinking. This is a wonderful Bard replacement for the usual few days of orientation for first year students. It was instituted some 35 years ago and is now a core part of the Bard experience, in which students not only focus on writing skills but also learn their way around campus and form new friendships before the start of school. The workshop involves a large dose of sophisticated reading material and very active class participation in small groups. It was, of course, important to have Conservatory students participate in the workshop, but the group from China would have been lost. Fortunately, I had near at hand a perfect solution! Katherine Gould-Martin, the managing director of Bard in China, agreed to teach a section of L&T (as it was known) consisting, that year, of the eight students from China. (In subsequent years her section included other Exception Admit students, notably from Hungary, the Czech Republic, Poland, Venezuela, South Korea, and Ukraine). Katherine came up with many ingenious and effective ways to provide the essential elements of the L&T program for these students, using small pieces of the readings and relying occasionally on explanations in Chinese. Thanks to her and the eagerness of most of the students, the program was a great success.

The Conservatory engaged an outside teacher for the special ESL class for our Exception Admit students, once the academic year began. This was, and has continued to be, a difficult class to teach. For one thing, the students' level varied widely; also, although the students surely realized the importance of the class, they were easily distracted by their musical activities combined, perhaps, with their sense that this was not a "real" course. Bard's professor of Chinese language and literature, Li-hua Ying, came to our rescue midway through the year and took over the ESL class. In our first 10 years we have had five different ESL teachers, each quite devoted and excellent and each reporting considerable frustrations and difficulties.

Figure 7 Lihua Ying and Katherine Gould-Martin

The first near-catastrophe occurred at the start of the second year of the Conservatory, in fall 2006, when the first group of Exception Admit students (all from China) enrolled in First-Year Seminar (FYS), one year late as planned, mixed in with regular first-year students in various sections of the course. Several of the FYS instructors raised concerns with the dean about the English language proficiency of the Chinese students, asking what was expected of them as instructors and expressing frustration with the teaching situation. Since these students had already completed a year of ESL training and were already a year late in taking FYS, and since the Conservatory was new, the situation was genuinely worrisome. Melvin Chen and I did feel that the reported difficulties were given special weight because the faculty and the dean considered them systemic—arising from the creation of the Conservatory—rather than simply as those normally encountered in the course of teaching.

When the problem reached the attention of Leon Botstein, he proposed a striking solution. Since the American students were reading the FYS works—for example the Greek classics, in translation—he suggested that we allow the Chinese students to read them in Chinese. He pointed out that the FYS course was about thinking, not about learning English; while the Chinese students would certainly need to improve their English, they should have the experience, as early as possible in their time at Bard, of engaging with the ideas of the great works. We happened to have on campus that year, as a visiting professor of history from Sun Yat Sen University in Guangzhou, a faculty member, Maybo Ching, whose Ph.D. was from Oxford University and who was able to teach a Chinese language section of FYS. Translations of the FYS works into Chinese were readily available—in fact, into both traditional and simplified characters. The arrangement had the additional advantage that the new group of first-year Exception Admit students from China could enter the course at once, instead of waiting until their second year. It allowed us to learn whether these students were up to the intellectual challenge of college academic work, without having to wait a year.

Some faculty of the College were shocked at this unconventional idea—the "great books" course taught in Mandarin—but the president prevailed. The course has continued to be offered every second year since then, with very good results. The teachers of the course have moved gradually to the use of English in the course of the year. This was certainly a key moment in the history of the Conservatory, in which the support and innovative ideas of Leon Botstein not only averted the crisis but also enhanced the daily workings of the Conservatory.

The problem of English language proficiency continues to be challenging. It is, in my view, a necessary problem, because the most gifted students in many parts of the world are encouraged to focus entirely on music. This is a feature of the very cultural bias that the Bard Conservatory challenges. We cannot avoid the problem by refusing to admit these students; rather, we need to admit them and then work with them to make it possible for them to succeed at Bard. Over the years we increased the intensity of the required ESL course, changing it from 4 to 8 credits. We also decided that at the end of that course students would need to satisfy a version of Bard's special "admission by essay" criterion before being allowed to register in courses that require a high level of English language proficiency.

This is perhaps also the place to mention the many success stories involving Conservatory students in the College. Not only have many Conservatory students turned out to be the among the very strongest in the College in their second majors, but it is frequently remarked that Conservatory students are models for other students in the areas of hard work, discipline, ambition, and accomplishment.

Recruitment in Hungary

Beginning with János Sutyák, a trombone player who came to Bard from a village near Debrecen in fall 2006, the number of Hungarian students in the Conservatory rose to 18 by 2012. This was due in large part to the extraordinary effort and genius of Olivia Cariño. The story of Olivia and her husband, László Z. Bitó '60 , needs to be told here. Their role in the Conservatory was transformative.

The story begins in December 1956, after the suppression of the Hungarian uprising by Soviet tanks and troops, when László and a group of approximately 300 Hungarian "Freedom Fighters" were invited to Bard College for a month of language study and orientation to the United States. At the end of that period, László and his fellow Hungarians delivered a proclamation expressing appreciation to the members of the Bard community "for the tremendous efforts exerted . . . to orient themselves to us Hungarian students." They conferred the title of "Honorary Hungarian College Professor" on the Bard faculty "who thought they could teach us the English language." László stayed on at Bard and graduated with a degree in biology in 1960. He earned his doctorate at Columbia in cell biology and biophysics, carried out research in London and again at Columbia, and rose through the ranks at Columbia to become professor of ocular physiology. He published more than 150 scientific articles, numerous reviews, and several scientific monographs. In 1994, at the age of 60, László published his first novel. Since then, in addition to patents for the eye-pressure-lowering glaucoma drug—Xalatan—he has gone on to publish eight more novels and five collections of essays.

In January 2007 Bard held a three-day conference and 50th reunion for the Hungarians who came to Bard in 1956. I met László and Olivia on the day before the opening of the conference in the midst of a fierce snowstorm. They agreed to hike through the snow to the music building to meet János Sutyák and to hear a sample of the playing of some of the Conservatory students. Our relationship developed from there. When Olivia heard that my next trip to Budapest for auditions for fall 2007 admission had gone badly (in fact, no one showed up, because of miscommunication), she took over the organization of the auditions. This included a concert in Budapest of current Conservatory students, a preconcert interview in a Budapest newspaper, a postconcert reception for members of the music community and the diplomatic corps, and well-publicized auditions, this time attended by some 40 applicants! In each subsequent year Olivia refined and improved the process, meeting with students in advance, helping in the preparation of audition materials, even finding Budapest-based Bard graduates to help Hungarian applicants prepare their application essays. In the meantime, the Bitós made a leadership gift toward matching our challenge grant from the Mellon Foundation, gave scholarship gifts for Hungarian students, and launched the Hungarian Visiting Fellows Program that for three years brought us scores of musicians, ranging from short-term visits from pianists Várjon Dénes and Izabella Simon, violist Peter Barsony, cellist István Varga, and flutist Gergy Ittzés to semester-long visits from then-students cellist Tamás Zétényi, violist David Toth, and bassist Bence Botar. The Bitós even purchased a contrabassoon in Budapest and paid for its seat on an airplane so that David Nagy, our bassoon student, could bring it to Bard! The story continues below.

Vocal Arts Program

Figure 8 Dawn Upshaw

In February 2004, before the opening of the Conservatory, I wrote to the soprano Dawn Upshaw to ask whether she would consider becoming involved, in any capacity. I had met Dawn after a concert she gave years before with Richard Goode at UCLA. I knew she was a great artist and I had heard wonderful things from many of my friends about her as a teacher and as a person. Dawn replied and suggested we meet to talk—it turned out that she received my letter around the same time that she had begun to think about the possibility of teaching, especially as her children were entering the later years of high school and she could imagine finding time in her schedule. Our conversation led to a meeting in the fall at Bard with Leon Botstein, in which we asked Dawn to assume the leadership of the vocal program in the Conservatory—either undergraduate or graduate, her choice. Dawn preferred the idea of creating a small graduate program. We settled on the idea that we would meet throughout that academic year—2005–06—to plan the program, and that the first students would be admitted in the fall of 2006. The meetings throughout that year—including Melvin Chen and Carol Yaple (Dawn's good friend and publicist) as well as Dawn and me—were exciting and productive, as Dawn thought through a program with a focus on art song, connections with text, work with theater directors, and including movement specialists and personalized career building in addition to the more customary parts of a vocal arts program (such as voice lessons and diction). Voice teachers were interviewed and hired, promotional materials were drafted and designed, and recruiting began in earnest. It became clear early on that an associate director was needed, partly because of Dawn's busy performance schedule, and a prime candidate emerged: Dawn's long-time associate in the Tanglewood summer voice program, the pianist and vocal coach Kayo Iwama. I traveled to Boston in the winter of 2006 to meet with Kayo and her husband, Frank Corliss, to try to recruit them to Bard. I was finally successful: Frank joined us to create and administer our new Postgraduate Collaborative Piano Fellows Program and to serve as staff pianist for the Conservatory, and he and Kayo were on campus for the opening of the program, along with our first eight vocal arts graduate students, in September 2006.[11]

Figure 9 A Vocal Arts graduate student with Kayo Iwama

[11] Added Fall 2019: Frank Corliss became director of the Conservatory and Stephanie Blythe became director of the Graduate Vocal Arts Program.

Figure 10 Frank Corliss

Enrollment growth

By 2015 the Conservatory had grown from 21 (in 2005) to 136 students, including undergraduates, certificate students, vocal arts students, and conducting students. In 2009 we received permission from the New York State Education Department to offer the certificate in Advanced Performance Studies (APS). That category has proven useful in cases where we were not satisfied with the pool of undergraduate applicants for particular instruments and were able to add highly qualified graduate students for two-year certificate programs of study. These APS graduate students participate fully in the instrumental studios, the orchestra, and the chamber music program of the Conservatory.[12] Beginning in fall 2006 we added eight students in the Graduate Vocal Arts Program, and another eight the following year. The target number of 16 students for this program has sometimes not been reached; in the Fall of 2015, however, 18 Vocal Arts students were enrolled.   Enrollment in the Graduate Conducting Program (Orchestral and Conducting tracks) has fluctuated around 10.

Within nine years of operation, 63 undergraduate students had completed the B. Music–B.A. program and graduated with the two degrees. By May 2020 that number climbed to 169.[13]

Space

In 2004, as plans for opening the Conservatory in Fall 2005 became definite, some last-minute modifications were made to the renovation of the Blum Building, home of the Music Program. In particular, a seminar room next to the Music Program chair's office was redesigned as an office for the

---

[12] Enrollment in the Conservatory's undergraduate and APS program grew from 21 in Fall 2005, as follows: 2006: 36; 2007: 53; 2008: 55; 2009: 73; 2010: 85; 2011: 90; 2012: 92; 2013: 98 ; 2014: 107. By Fall 2020, 119 undergraduates and APS students were enrolled.

[13] By May 2020 there were 88 graduates of the Graduate Vocal Arts program; 50 graduates of the Graduate Conducting Program; 66 graduates of the APS program; 30 graduates of the Graduate Piano Fellows program.

director of the Conservatory and part of the outer office space was assigned to Conservatory use. Beyond that, Melvin Chen had a piano studio in Blum. When the Graduate Vocal Arts Program opened in fall 2006, the Ward Manor Gatehouse, previously the site of two small faculty apartments, was given over to the use of that program.

That was the situation for the first seven years of the Conservatory, even as it doubled and tripled in size—the Vocal Arts Program was separated from the rest of the Conservatory, which itself shared space with the Music Program of the College. Master classes and graduation recitals were held in Olin Auditorium, a hall of about 400 seats in the center of campus, or in Blum Hall or Bard Hall, performance spaces with a capacity of about 50.

In spring 2009 Leon Botstein returned from a trip to Budapest with the exciting news that László Bitó had offered to help the Conservatory with its space problem. I think he had heard about our space problems from students, through his wife Olivia. Throughout the summer of 2010 I worked with the campus architect, Robert Nilsson, on ideas for a new Conservatory wing of the existing Blum Music Building. In October I traveled to Budapest with Debra Pemstein, Bard's vice president for development and alumni/ae affairs, bringing a photo album on the history of the Conservatory since 2005 and a set of schematic architectural drawings and cost estimates for a possible new wing. Together we made a presentation to the Bitós. László had a number of questions and ideas and we agreed to pursue these, with cost options, as soon as we returned to Bard. In the next days I held auditions in Budapest, and on the day I left Olivia sent me an e-mail, thanking us for sharing our plans and saying there was "still much homework left to do." She was looking forward to hearing about details and options.

By early December 2010, I was able to send László answers, with cost estimates, to the questions he raised. Olivia wrote that they would call me in a few days, after their meeting with Leon in Budapest. On the morning of December 10, I received Leon's report of the meeting at which the Bitós agreed to a gift of $9.2 million for construction of the new Conservatory home. I wrote to Olivia and László : "I just woke up but I think I'm still dreaming. I read Leon's report of this meeting with you. I'm thrilled beyond words and filled with gratitude and excitement. I'll write again when I calm down."

Things moved quickly. On January 21, 2011, the trustees of the College approved the construction of the building by the architect Deborah Berke and Associates, with a start date in September 2011 and completion by December 2012. A groundbreaking ceremony took place on Bard's Family Weekend on October 28, 2011. We moved into the new space on schedule in January 2013, finally bringing together the Graduate Vocal Arts Program with the rest of the Conservatory. The formal opening, attended by the Bitós, the architect, and many other guests, took place on April 8, 2013. It included the reading of a celebratory poem by Robert Kelly and a performance of a Bach work for chorus and instruments. The building includes 15 teaching studios, a main office, an elegant lobby, and a beautiful performance space. The rooms have marvelous acoustics; the halls and rooms are light filled and attractive. The effect on the Conservatory has been simply wonderful.

Figure 11 Inspecting the new Bito Conservatory Building

Figure 12 Atrium of the Bito Conservatory Building

Figure 13 The Laszlo Bito Conservatory Building

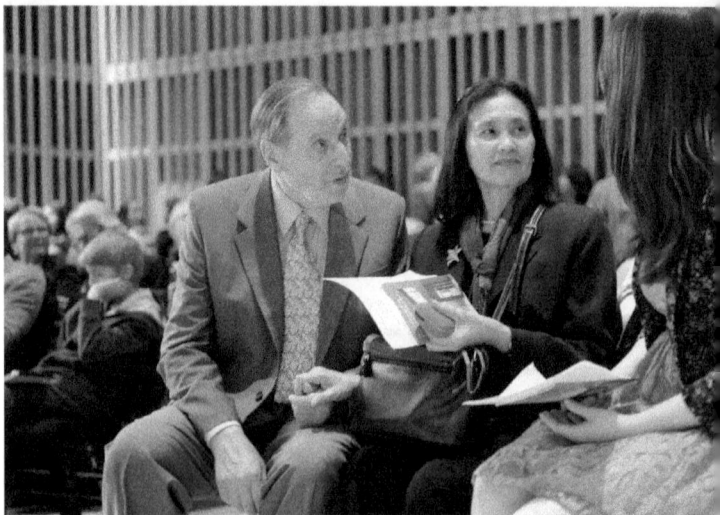

Figure 14 Laszlo and Olivia Bito at the opening celebration

The Orchestra Program

In the first years of the Conservatory, the orchestra (actually a chamber orchestra in those days) was assembled twice each semester, with rehearsals clustered in the period before the concert. Only later, as our numbers increased, and when Botstein became music director of the orchestra and Erica Kiesewetter joined us as director of orchestral studies, did the orchestra become a regular program with twice-weekly rehearsals and four main programs each year. Botstein generally conducts two of the concerts each season; guest conductors have included Fabio Machetti, Harold Farberman, Xian Zhang, Michael

Gilbert, Guillermo Figueroa, Nanse Gum, David Alan Miller, Gisele Ben-Dor, Rossen Milanov, Marcelo Lehninger, and Cristian Maceleru.

Since October 2010 the orchestra has performed every year at Eastern Correctional Facility in Napanoch, New York, a maximum security prison. This was first arranged in May 2010 when I attended a graduation ceremony for the Bard Prison Initiative at Eastern. I was in conversation after the ceremony with the superintendent of that prison and Leon Botstein. One of us remarked that the auditorium would be suitable for a concert and Leon suggested that we bring our orchestra to perform. It was arranged for the following fall. The orchestra manager, Fu-chen Chan, had to make an advance trip with Max Kenner, head of the Bard Prison Initiative; as I recall, she took along a cello as a sample of an instrument that would have to pass through the security check. We brought two busloads of students, preceded by a truck with timpani, harp, other percussion instruments, and 90 music stands.

The students were nervous and excited as they arrived for the preconcert rehearsal. Cell phones, wallets, keys—everything—had to be left in the bus, and each student and guest went through an elaborate check-in and metal-detector scan, and received a fluorescent mark on the wrist. When the halls were cleared of inmates we were escorted to the auditorium. The room had a metallic, dry acoustic, not unlike many high school auditoriums. The orchestra squeezed onto the stage, basses and percussion hardly visible at the back edges.

When it was time for the concert the inmates were brought in, filing into seats at the back and middle of the auditorium, leaving a gap of about 15 rows behind the guests in the front six or eight rows. The students were dressed in concert clothes—men in tuxedos, women in black dresses. The program began with words of introduction by the prison superintendent, followed by greetings and explanatory comments by Leon Botstein on the pieces to be played. The students played with intensity. The fans in the room had been turned off to reduce the noise, and as the heat rose the students' faces glowed with perspiration. The applause after each piece was thunderous. There were three works—a Rossini overture, the Ferdinand David Trombone Concerto, and a Dvořák symphony. When the concert ended, Botstein took questions from the inmates. Each questioner began with words of appreciation for the performance. How were the pieces selected? How did students come to choose the instruments they played? How was it different to play in a prison? One inmate asked, where would his children be able to hear this kind of music?

Figure 15 Performance at Eastern Correctional Facility

We had arranged for dinner after the concert for the orchestra and guests, including officials from the prison, at a large nearby restaurant. We had the restaurant to ourselves and it turned into quite a wonderful event. The mood was warm and jovial, the food was ample and good, the conversation was animated, and there were many rounds of congratulations and applause for the various speeches and announcements. Then students boarded the buses for the ride back to Bard, arriving there around midnight.

The prison concert has turned out to be a much-anticipated annual event, each time followed by dinner at the same restaurant. Several years after her graduation from Bard, one of our students, a violinist who went on to postgraduate study at Curtis, commented to me, in the midst of negative comments about a recent concert experience she had had at a prestigious summer festival, that the most satisfying concert experiences she had ever had were the prison concerts during her years at Bard.

In May 2010, to celebrate the Conservatory's fifth birthday, the orchestra played in Alice Tully Hall in New York's Lincoln Center. Chen was soloist in George Perle's second piano concerto, and Dawn Upshaw was soloist in the Fourth Symphony of Mahler. To bring the orchestra to full size we included a substantial number of "ringers," as we also did for rehearsals and concerts throughout the year. The concert was very favorably reviewed in the *New York Times*, though the critic felt called upon to note the number—and, as I recall, even gave an exact count—of the nonstudents in the orchestra. In each subsequent year the number of ringers has decreased, and by the time of our summer 2014 European tour there were only three ringers (though we did bring along a number of recent graduates to fill out the string violin and viola sections). In 2011 the orchestra played at Sanders Theater at Harvard University; in June 2012 it made a three-week tour of greater China: Taipei, Hong Kong, Shanghai, Beijing, Tianjin, Guangzhou, and Wuhan. In May 2013 the orchestra returned to Alice Tully Hall, this time for a concert that included performances of the first Prokofiev Violin Concerto, with Bard faculty member Shmuel

Ashkenasi as soloist, and the Shostakovich Symphony No. 5. In June 2014, the orchestra toured Eastern Europe and Russia, with performances in great and historic halls in Warsaw, St. Petersburg (the Mariinsky concert hall), Moscow (the Great Hall of the Tchaikovsky Conservatory), Budapest (the Great Hall of the Franz Liszt Academy), Bratislava (the concert hall of Slovakia Radio), Vienna (the Konzerthaus), Prague (the Rudolfinum) and Berlin (the Berlin Konzerthaus).

Figure 16 Bard Conservatory Orchestra in Prague

Figure 17 Bard Conservatory Orchestra at Harvard's Sanders Theater

The Chamber Music Program

Melvin Chen and I placed considerable importance on developing a strong chamber music program in the Conservatory. There are structural factors that make this somewhat difficult: the groups generally change from semester to semester, rehearsals are scheduled by the groups themselves, and there are not the large group performances and tours that build the morale of an orchestra or a chorus. In my own conservatory experience, chamber music was definitely secondary in the curriculum—rehearsals and coaching sessions were rescheduled or cancelled to make room for other priorities. We tried to meet these difficulties in several ways: we required chamber music in every semester for every student, we organized frequent chamber music master classes by visiting artists to raise the visibility of the program, we provided funds on several occasions to support participation in the finals of national chamber music competitions, and perhaps most importantly, we organized many outside performance opportunities for "mixed" groups of faculty and students playing together. We adopted the policy that all groups would have a performance opportunity toward the end of each semester, but that for the outside engagements of the mixed groups, the choice of players would be "non-democratic" – i.e., based entirely on the student's level of playing. Faculty-student groups performed at the Library of Congress, the Rhinebeck Chamber Music Society, the Reading Pennsylvania Chamber Music Society, the American Philosophical Society in Philadelphia, the Greenwich Music School in New York City, in Shanghai and Beijjing, and in a tour that included Budapest, Vienna, Bratislava, Brno, and Prague. One student quartet that formed in the first year of the Conservatory stayed together for five years, survived a few changes in personnel, called itself the Chimeng Quartet (from "Qimeng," the Chinese word for "enlightenment," a major theme of the First-Year Seminar), and achieved considerable success, including an invitation to perform at the Shanghai World Expo in 2010 and winning the Silver Medal at the Fischoff Chamber Music Competition. The Chimeng Quartet received considerable publicity, including a front page profile in the U.S. edition of *China Daily*. Another student group, the Hudson Valley Brass Quintet, capped off a successful season of performances with two weeks as an invited ensemble at the Stellenbosch Chamber Music Festival in South Africa.

Figure 18 At the University of Hong Kong: Weigang Li, Dongfang Ouyang, Robert Martin, Rylan Gajek-Leonard, Melvin Chen, Lin Wang

The cumulative effect of these activities has been as hoped, a strong presence of chamber music in the life of the Conservatory. Many groups stay together from semester to semester. A marathon concert starting at 1 p.m. in the afternoon, with a break for supper (with the audience) and continuing late into the evening, is needed at the end of each semester to accommodate the performances of the ensembles of that semester.

Fund raising

Figure 19 Robert Martin speaking to Conservatory donors

In 2005 the Conservatory received an "Implementation Grant" of $230,000 (divided over three years) from The Andrew W. Mellon Foundation—a follow up to the $40,000 Planning Grant of 2004. In 2008 I visited the Mellon

Foundation's new president, Don Randel, along with officers of the Foundation's Liberal Arts Colleges Program, to describe the progress of the Conservatory and the use we had made of the earlier Mellon Foundation support. The outcome of this meeting was an invitation to submit a proposal for an endowment challenge grant, restricted to support of the "core undergraduate academic program." As part of the Mellon's consideration of that proposal, we were asked to confirm that we would not depart from our commitment to the double-degree requirement, and that we would strive to enroll more (and a higher percentage) of U.S. students. I believe this second point was based on the view at the Foundation that U.S. students would in general be better prepared for the academic part of the double-degree program; perhaps they were also concerned that the difficulties described above in connection with the English language proficiency of the international students might impede or even sink the double-degree program. We made both commitments.

I was also asked, during consideration of our proposal, what level of matching funds we could commit to. It was clear in this connection that at least a 1:1 match would be required, and that agreement to a match beyond 1:1 would be welcomed and would strengthen our proposal. In my enthusiasm (and naivete?) I agreed to a match as high as 3:1—that we would raise $3 for every $1 from the Foundation. In

2008 we were awarded a $2.5 million grant to be used as endowment for the Conservatory's core undergraduate academic program (not to be used for financial aid) on condition that we raise three times that amount, i.e., $7.5 million within four years.[14] Due to the 2008 downturn of the economy, we were unable to make the first deadline (September, 2012) for raising those matching funds—we had raised approximately $2 million by that time. We requested and were granted a four-year extension of the deadline, this time to September 2016.[15]

Our Conservatory remains a work in progress, so this brief history ends with only a few simple reflections, no grand conclusion.

The arrival of each new student brings the excitement of a promise to be kept. Each graduation recital reveals a miracle of growth. Each master class, orchestra performance, and chamber music concert brings pride and, to be honest, a certain incredulousness that our Conservatory is as real and successful as it has become. Each day of work with

---

14 The arrangement was this: the $2.5 million was transferred to the College with the understanding that as increments of $100,000 (cash, not pledges) were placed in a Conservatory endowment fund, $33,333 of Mellon Foundation funds would also be added to that endowment fund and the interest on those combined endowment funds would be available to the Conservatory.

15 [Added in 2020] A second extension was granted, to December 31, 2018. That deadline was met, providing the Conservatory with an endowment of $10 million.

our amazing staff fills me with admiration and gratitude for the hard work accomplished so well, with dedication and, above all, with love for our students.

Added in 2020

There have of course been many important developments in the years since this brief history was written in 2015. I will mention just two, the creation of the US-China Music Institute in 2017, through which the Conservatory now includes instruction in traditional Chinese instruments in its double degree undergraduate program, and the Conservatory's new leadership as of July 2019.

To explain how the Bard Conservatory came to have a US-China Music Institute, I need to begin with some personal remarks. The story starts for me in Fall 1972 when my wife, Katherine, and I and our two children, age 4 and 3, lived in a farmhouse in rural Taiwan, a walk of about 20 minutes from the small market town of Shu-lin. We were there because Katherine was pursuing field work for her PhD dissertation in anthropology. I remember being awakened by the piercing, mournful sounds of an instrument that I couldn't identify, somewhere between a trumpet and an oboe. Katherine told me it is was part of a funeral procession, and indeed I caught a glimpse of the procession of mourners wearing burlap shawls and hoods through the window of our second story rooms. The procession was accompanied by the sounds of percussion instruments and the suona, which I later learned was the name of the main instrument. I thought the sound was extraordinary, especially when I realized that it went on continuously for impossibly long stretches. I became mesmerized waiting to hear a break in the sound (for a breath), until I realized that I was hearing circular breathing – air taken in while air in the cheeks propelled the sound.

This was my introduction to Chinese music, some 58 years ago, supplemented by hearing performances of Chinese opera on small wooden stages set up in the fields near our house to celebrate various gods' birthdays.

Bard's connections with China developed through years of exploration. The Bard-in-China program was active since 1999, many years before the founding of the Bard Conservatory, sponsoring events and exchanges with scholars and institutions in China and elsewhere in Asia. The Conservatory was, from its earliest years, enriched by the presence of distinguished faculty and wonderfully gifted students from China. These embers were fanned when, at the suggestion of my old friend, Jindong Cai, we hosted the Chamber Orchestra of the Forbidden City, from Beijing, to play at Bard in February 2017. I was so impressed by the beauty of the playing - the refinement and virtuosity – and I was particularly impressed by the fact that half of the music on the program was recently composed. I realized, what I should have known already, that a Chinese instrument ensemble was not only for the performance of ancient works but also for every kind of contemporary music. I was reminded then of fascinating new works I had heard over the years for combinations of Chinese and Western instruments, for example by Chen Yi, and by our 2010 composition graduate Yiwen Shen.

Figure 20 Jindong Cai

We decided to create the US-China Music Institute partly because we saw the opportunity and couldn't resist it! We realized that we could, through our connections with colleagues in China, find wonderful faculty including visiting professors from the Central Conservatory of Music. We saw that we wouldn't have to change the core of our curriculum to accommodate Chinese-instrument majors, since they would join all the other students in the double-degree program. We were assured that the opportunity to attend the Bard Conservatory would be attractive to high-level Chinese-instrument students in China, knowing that they would have great teachers and the chance to have a first-class western-style liberal arts education. We felt confident that before long our program would attract non-Chinese students to the study of Chinese instruments.

Another motivation was that we could distinguish ourselves by being the first conservatory in the U.S., perhaps the first anywhere outside of Asia, with Chinese-instrument majors. A young conservatory such as Bard needs to find ways to distinguish itself whenever possible.

In September 2017 the conductor, educator and writer Jindong Cai joined Bard as director of the US-China Music Institute and professor of arts. In December 2017 we traveled together to Beijing where Yu Feng, president of the Central Conservatory of Music, and I signed a comprehensive agreement for the development of Chinese music at Bard. In the short time since signing that agreement, the Institute has hosted major festivals, conferences, a summer study program, and, most importantly, brought the study of Chinese instruments, and the wonderful sounds of these instruments, into the daily life of the Conservatory.

Figure 21 Jindong Cai, Yu Feng, Robert Martin

Figure 22 2017 High School Program students

At the end of June 2019, I stepped down as director of the Bard Conservatory. My colleague, Frank Corliss, who had served since 2014 as associate director, became director. A new position, dean of the Conservatory, was created, and the distinguished composer Tan Dun agreed to fill that position. This new team took over the leadership of the Conservatory in July 2019. It is the Conservatory's extraordinary good fortune to have the combination of Frank Corliss, who knows every aspect of the Conservatory from the inside, and has already contributed so much to its success, and Tan Dun, who brings, from the outside, vibrant new ideas and international acclaim. It will be exciting to watch what they do, and even better for the generations of new students who will benefit from their leadership and dedication.

Figure 23Tan Dun with students

Chapter Four

Reflections of Bard Conservatory Graduates

In the summer of 2020, graduates of the Bard Conservatory from the years 2010-2019 were invited to reflect on their experiences as undergraduate students, particularly with respect to the double-degree aspect of its curriculum. I received the following, presented here in alphabetical order.

Xiao Chen '12, piano, went on from Bard to The Juilliard School and then to UCLA where she completed the DMA in 2017. She is now a member of the faculty of Mount Saint Mary's University in Los Angeles. At Bard, her second major was French Studies, with a senior project entitled "*Aller et Retours Littéraires*: Franco-Chinese Literary Connections from Voltaire to Gao Xingjian."

At Bard we were required to choose another major outside music and arts — I chose French. During my years at Bard I spent innumerable days practicing till midnight; I had to juggle piano practice with classes, readings, and papers. I initially groused about this, but soon afterwards I retracted my grievances.The readings and discussions influenced my practice. I still recall many distinctive moments: experiments in the physics lab for an acoustics class, discussions regarding slaves and freedom in a sociopolitical class, research for my paper that explored the lives of "barbarians" in European history, and the study of Baudelaire's *Les Fleur du mal* in the French literature class. These non-music classes encouraged me in independent and creative thinking; they shaped my artistry and gave me intellectual strength and confidence. They developed my multidimensional thinking about music.

In addition to scholarly inspiration, the professional music training at the Bard Conservatory guided me to find my distinctive path in music. The Conservatory strongly advocated chamber music and I had opportunities to work closely, and to perform, with faculty. I had the honor to study piano with professor Melvin Chen; had regular masterclasses with Richard Goode and Peter Serkin, and received chamber music coachings from many world-class musicians. The environment was very friendly; the professors took care of students like family. The regular meetings with advisers and with our director Mr. Martin helped us throughout. Bard improved my approach to music, to be able to see beyond the notes and the analysis of chords to the world beyond the score. I am sincerely grateful to the Bard

Conservatory, to Bard College, and to all the professors who were part of my journey.

Xuanbo (Kang) Dong '14, oboe, went on from Bard for an MBA at the IESE Business School in Barcelona, Spain. His second major at Bard was Political Studies, with a senior project entitled "Amid the River Currents."

What is the point of having a second major for a musician?

How does reading Kafka's *Metamorphosis* and Darwin's *On the Origin of Species* improve my playing of the Strauss Oboe Concerto? Don't things like that only take away valuable time from practicing? When my father caught me reading Dante in Chinese when I was fourteen, he merely frowned and groaned "Go practice!".

"Well, if I keep up with my practice, learning more surely wouldn't hurt?" I reasoned.

I took a full course load every semester at Bard and tried to soak up as much knowledge as I could. I pursued my interest in political studies and chose it as my second major, initiating a series of endless political debates with my classmates. I took classes in comparative literature and economics, and joined a study-abroad program in Hungary. Propelled by my love for European opera and literature, I learned Italian and French, then wrote poems in those languages for *Sui Generis*, the Bard poetry journal.

"The world is bigger than you," my adviser at Bard used to tell me. Only much later did I come to realize the truth that lies in that cliché-sounding statement. One can hardly appreciate the breathtaking vastness of the world if one only looks at what is at hand.

Later, lured by the promise of a handsome income in the business world, I entered IESE, a business school in Barcelona, Spain. The admission officer laughed as she told me the school probably never had an oboist with a conservatory degree among its students. Although surrounded by managers, consultants, and investment bankers, I declined to follow the business school craze of applying for jobs at MBB, Goldman Sachs and Morgan Stanley. I knew that a life in finance would never be bearable for me, and that I would return to music, where I started. I decided to help my father with his oboe business in China, and now I am a musical instrument dealer. Traveling from a trade show in Shanghai to a music festival in Granada, from a music conference in Florida to instrument shops in Paris, I find the same thrill in the moment of sale as I did on stage. If I could go back in time and face the ardent and impetuous youth that was my former self, I would tell him to open his eyes to the world to learn as much as he could. Knowledge enriches one's soul, enables one to better grasp the beauty of the world and, ultimately, grants a more fulfilling existence.

Felicia Doni '17, piano.   Second major was Human Rights, with a senior project entitled "Art and Resistance in Moldova: Bessarabia's Politically Troubled Emergence Toward National Identity Reflected in the Story of Musicians Ion and Doina Aldea-Teodorovici."

I first remember meeting my conservatory class at Mr. Martin's house, where he invited us for brunch on a sunny, fall, Sunday morning the day before classes began. There, as we exchanged friendly "Hellos";"What instrument do you play?" "Where are you from?" – the seeds of camaraderie were planted. For the next five years of our lives, we would accompany each other through the ups and downs of college life, forming forever friendships.

My experience at Bard was a dream come true. The double-degree program offered endless opportunities to grow musically, intellectually, and personally. Both academically and musically, I grew into my interests and also had the chance to explore new ones. As I took classes at the college and conservatory, I discovered fascinating connections across disciplines, art forms, and modes of thought. As a pianist, I had the privilege of studying with the great Peter Serkin, as well as partaking in masterclasses with visiting artists of the highest caliber. In the College, I pursued my interest in social justice initiatives and chose Human Rights as my major.

Two of the most unique aspects of Bard Conservatory, I believe, are its culture of mutual support among students, and its emphasized value of creating meaningful music, thoughtfully. There was a sense of solidarity among us all, perhaps strengthened by the bond we shared in unanimously participating in a challenging double degree program. The freedom to explore one's intellectual proclivities – an innate attribute of the liberal arts model – reflected in a freedom of musical expression and exploration. Being exposed to a broad range of subjects resulted in a widened perspective and scope of music making. We were all encouraged, either explicitly by our instructors or implicitly through our parallel learning, to carefully consider the music we created, to challenge the standard ways, to self-examine, to try novel approaches, to see another way, to communicate. We were there to make meaningful connections through our playing, not to compete against one another.

Many of the greatest musicians were (and are) great thinkers. The Bard Conservatory provides the luxury of exploring your own freedom of thought, a privilege that is often undervalued. I could not have imagined a richer experience than my five years at Bard. Today, I teach piano in Portland, Oregon while also performing piano. Ultimately, I hope to contribute to efforts in environmental justice in the Pacific Northwest, while continuing to collaborate on musical projects with my Bard Conservatory family, now spread wide across the world.

Greg Drilling '16, oboe, is a vice president at a leading global public affairs consulting firm in New York City. His second major at Bard was Political Studies and he also studied Chinese. His senior project was entitled, "Presidential Power in Foreign Policy: Richard Nixon and the Era of Détente with the Soviet Union and China."

My journey to Bard is a bit unconventional. Before attending Bard, I spent my first year of college studying oboe performance at a leading New York City music conservatory, whose curriculum was exclusively music related. Towards the end of my first semester, I began to wish I had the opportunity to take non-music-related courses. I always had a strong interest in politics, history, and foreign languages. Early in my second semester, my oboe professor told me about the Bard Conservatory and its unique double-degree program. I soon realized that much of Bard's faculty also taught at leading conservatories in New York, and I was attracted to the performance opportunities I would be able to partake in.

I transferred to Bard in the Fall of 2012, and I couldn't have been happier with my decision. The emphasis on studying music within the context of a liberal education while having access to and instruction from world-class faculty was incredibly rewarding. I can't think of any other institution in the world that provides an education like Bard. The opportunities available to me were truly life changing.

I ultimately decided that I wanted to pursue a career in politics rather than music. After graduating in 2016, I was offered a job at a political fundraising consulting firm in New York City, where I worked on the campaigns of multiple members of Congress and the New York State Legislature. In September 2017, I was offered a job on the re-election campaign for New York State Governor Andrew Cuomo. Following the Governor's successful re-election in November 2018, I was offered a position at a leading global public affairs consulting firm in New York City, where I currently serve as a vice president. My work focuses on government affairs, public affairs, and strategic communications consulting for corporations, nonprofit organizations, leading advocacy groups, governments, NGOs, and prominent public and political figures.

I'm also very fortunate to be a member of an orchestra in New York composed of dedicated, serious, and like-minded musicians who want to perform in an ensemble at a high level, but who chose not to pursue a career in music performance. Members of the orchestra hail from the most prestigious conservatories in the country, and we are currently led by Maestro David Chan, Concertmaster of the Metropolitan Opera Orchestra.

I think that the mission of the Bard Conservatory is something that still applies to my life today. My Bard education taught me how to think outside the box, pursue my interests, and that it's okay not to limit myself to just one thing. If you're passionate about something, it can always be a part of your life.

Emanuel Evans '10, cello, is Senior Software Engineer at Rainforest QA and continues to perform, especially in the San Francisco Bay area. After Bard, Emanuel pursued a master's degree at the New England Conservatory. His second major at Bard was Political Studies, with a senior project on the strong influence of Christian Zionism in shaping U.S. policy toward Israel.

The first thing I remember from my time at Bard was the visceral feeling of jumping into the unknown. The day I arrived on campus, I knew that not only was I entering a new chapter in my personal life, but I was also participating in the inaugural year of a radical new experiment in musical education—the mandatory double-degree program.

Throughout my time at Bard, that feeling of discovery never really went away. Something about the atmosphere encouraged constant exploration and experimentation, and I quickly got addicted to the feeling of always trying something new, even if it came with some mild chaos (and it often did!). Whether it was spending a semester in Budapest, trying (and failing) to learn Arabic over a summer in Morocco, studying international relations in New York, or even trying my hand at composing, I always jumped at the opportunity to try something out of the ordinary. The difference I felt when attending a "traditional" conservatory for graduate school was stark: I often felt stifled by the "normal" way of doing things that had been built up over decades, and I missed the seemingly endless opportunities for learning that came with the double-degree program.

Since graduating, my career has taken some twists and turns. I'm not working day-to-day in either politics or music (my Bard degrees) and have instead drifted into software engineering. But the constant need for discovery has never really gone away. A few years ago I joined a startup with seven employees and was plunged into that familiar feeling of mild chaos and uncertainty that I remember from my freshman year at Bard. I don't think I'll ever really be able to live without that feeling for very long.

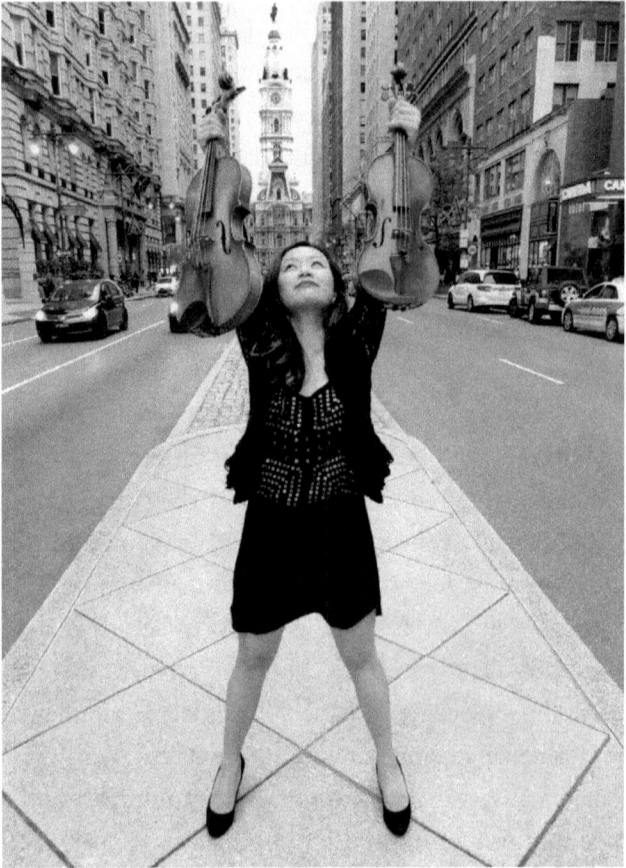

Luosha Fang '13, violin, went on from Bard to the Curtis Institute and later to the Reina Sofia Academy in Madrid where she studied viola with Nobuko Imai. She won first prize in the 2018 Tokyo International Viola Competition, and first prize in the 2019 Classic Strings International Competition in Vienna. Her second major at Bard was Russian Studies, with a senior project comparing Pushkin's and Tchaikovsky's treatment of the figure of Eugene Onegin.

As a classical musician, I always try to search for ways to connect with others through the language of music. It is often challenging to accomplish my goal. Often when I have difficult moments, I think back to my time at the Bard Conservatory of Music. I am truly grateful that I had the opportunity to meet Mr. Robert Martin and Katherine there. As a teenager who arrived directly from Shanghai to this foreign land, I was immediately welcomed and guided by these superb human beings. They showed me by example how important it is to care about our communities, environment, animals and the younger generation. To this day, I often think about how they would act in various situations in dealing with political and social issues.

My years at Bard were filled with intellectual stimulation and generosity from my mentors and friends. My most vivid memories include performing concerts in many states with my string quartet (Chimeng String Quartet) and Mr. Martin. On campus, I was inspired to think critically through diverse courses in the humanities, sciences and arts. I also had opportunities for intimate discussions with my professors and classmates. Everyone I encountered was progressive, democratic and an independent thinker. I really thought that was the norm in the United States. Idealism is not simply a philosophical approach in life. It is also achievable at a place called Bard.

As a performing musician, I believe that the double-degree program is crucial for the younger generation to be able to incorporate art into the society. It allows future musicians to have more dimensions in their artistry and possibly produces future music supporters as well. Bard indeed made me who I am both as a person and as an artist.

Leah Rose Gastler '11, viola, went on to Juilliard, to Rice University's Shepherd School of Music, and then to the creation of her own "visibility coaching" company, Leah Rose. Her second major at Bard was Latin American and

Iberian Studies, with a senior project that was a translation and analysis of poems by the Chilean poet Delia Dominguez.

I arrived at Bard at a time in my life when my academic interests were expanding. After focusing so intently on landing a spot in a top conservatory, I had begun to be curious about the world beyond classical music. Bard's program was brand new: no legacy, no shiny name like the other schools I was applying to. But it had a unique premise that captivated me: world-class classical music education in the context of the liberal arts.

The feeling at Bard was expansive. The mandate of the double degree was bold and intimidating, but also an *opportunity*. I had access to every department of study I could imagine, and any course that piqued my interest: thoughtful experts in every field who would illuminate and supplement my understanding and connection to the world of music. Bard's premise was unprecedented and challenging: that we as classical musicians *should* immerse ourselves in the liberal arts alongside our necessarily intense musical study, so that we could fully understand its relevance in the historical and current context of our world.

What I appreciated most about my experience at Bard was the recognition that each student has a unique path, as artist, student, and individual. Individuality was fostered in a way that was both empowering and challenging: we forged our own academic paths, created our own course selections, chose our second major, paced the balance of senior project with senior recital, met the demands and made them our own, over the course of 5 years. This required us to step up as leaders in our own lives, to shape the trajectory of our education and curate our own experience of inquiry and insight.

At Bard, it was understood that we weren't just learning to be classical musicians: we were diverse *people* in the study of music, connecting our music with the world and our experience of life, and really allowing the two to interact. As we studied philosophy, literature, and anthropology, we learned more about ourselves, and we channeled all of this through our music. Through the liberal arts, we could understand that music doesn't exist in a vacuum. It cannot stand alone, without the history, culture, and context of our world. It shifts as our world shifts and evolves as we evolve. Music as our expression is inextricably tied to our human experience. At Bard, we had the opportunity to learn that for ourselves.

After Bard, I went on to study at The Juilliard School and Rice University's Shepherd School of Music. And through the variety of models of conservatory education that I have been privileged to experience, I've continued to forge my own purpose-aligned path in my music and life. I started a non-profit music festival in my hometown of Durham, CT, where we host world-class chamber music concerts in a garden setting. In addition to freelancing throughout the country, I take pride and joy in being a career coach for classical musicians, helping them improve their performance confidence, visibility, and creative expression to build a thriving career as an embodiment of their true purpose in life. My understanding of what it means to be a fulfilled person in music is thanks to the foundation I received at Bard: we are a whole world - a unique purpose and passion in search of expression through music and life.

Jimmy Haber '14, French horn, worked for the Alibaba Group for three years before joining the startup Thunkable, a platform for building mobile apps. His second major at Bard was Asian Studies, with a senior project entitled "A Case Study of Civil Diplomacy: The American Chamber of Commerce in the People's Republic of China."

As a double-degree student at Bard College, I was encouraged to pursue my interests in music and academics at the highest level. In the Conservatory, my French horn teachers, chamber coaches, and music professors were all top players and leading music scholars. And while they provided terrific technical training, they were also just as interested in my personal growth. The care and dedication of the faculty created a warm and serious atmosphere where young musicians could thrive.

Bard's double-degree program attracts some of the brightest and most talented musicians from around the world. Post-rehearsal hangouts could easily (and frequently did) turn into long discussions about our other areas of study. One hour you're rehearsing Brahms, and the next your friend who plays bassoon and studies biology is explaining how the fruit you eat is the ripened ovary of a plant.

Most importantly, my academic degree in the college was encouraged and seen as an integral part of my development as a musician. I was constantly pushed to consider the interconnectedness of music with the rest of the world. In the college, my advisor and professors helped me focus my interests on US-China relations. For years, I was carefully guided each semester to deepen my understanding of Asian history, politics, economics, and anthropology. This included a rigorous study of Mandarin Chinese, which brought me to China for two summers through Bard's language exchange program with Qingdao University.

After graduation, I interned with the National Committee on US-China Relations in New York City, before moving to San Francisco to work for Alibaba

Group. I spent the next three years traveling between San Francisco and China, working with Alibaba's International Corporate Affairs team. After working at Alibaba Group and seeing how technology was enabling non-technical business owners, I joined a Y-Combinator-backed startup called Thunkable to manage their user operations and communications functions. Through Thunkable I have continued to travel to China, now as a judge for app building competitions for Chinese high school students.

While I decided to pursue my academic degree as a career, music continues to be an active part of my life. I regularly play French horn and trumpet with several San Francisco-based music ensembles, and in 2019 I wrote and performed an original rap version of Prokofiev's "Peter and the Wolf," with the San Francisco Civic Symphony and several Bay Area-based rappers. I'm not sure if that's what Prokofiev intended, but I think he would have enjoyed the performance.

Like everyone else quarantined around the world right now because of COVID-19, I am unsure what the future holds. But I'm confident that with the skills and interests I cultivated through the double-degree program at Bard, I will continue to pursue interesting and meaningful projects with intense drive and creativity.

Photo credit: Deanna Ng

Frances Lee '14, piano, went on from Bard to the Shepherd School of Music at Rice University where she completed the DMA degree in Piano Performance in 2020. She is now a member of the faculty at a tertiary-level institution in Singapore. Her second major at Bard was German Studies, with a senior project entitled "Italy, Writing and Music: A Translation with a Critical Introduction of Fanny Mendelssohn-Hensel's *Italienisches Tagebuch* **(Italian Diary).**

Bard magnified my love of learning and reinforced my belief in the importance of a holistic education. I did not truly understand the power of a liberal arts education until I studied there, and I have appreciated it more and more as I continue my journey in the realm of education, first as a student through my master's and doctoral degree programs, and now as a faculty member at a tertiary-level institution. The critical thinking and communication skills nurtured through discussion- and writing-based classes are more important than ever in today's society, not least for musicians and artists who need to navigate a time when traditional career paths are increasingly difficult to pursue. Flexibility of thought and the ability to delve into different fields of knowledge enable our engagement in interdisciplinary work, crucial at a time of increasing specialization. These skills are far from abstract, but instead inform everything in my life: the outreach projects that I carry out as a performer, the way that I communicate with my students as a teacher, and even the way that I approach the television shows that I watch.

Equally important to my undergraduate experience was the support and loving encouragement that I was fortunate to receive from faculty, staff, and fellow students. At this formative time, it was freeing to know that there was a safe space for creativity, and being able to run my own projects built an independence that has served me well. I went to Bard for its belief that musicians need to learn about more than music, and left shaped in ways that I will continue to treasure. I look back on my time there with great fondness and gratitude, and I now strive to create a similar experience for my students.

Shun-Yang Lee '11, piano, received his PhD in Information Systems from the University of Texas, Austin. He is now assistant professor of marketing at Northeastern University's D'Amore-McKim School of Business in Boston. His second major at Bard was mathematics, and his senior project was entitled, "Time-Frequency Analysis of the Shepard Tone."

The double-degree program at the Bard Conservatory requires that students pursue a music degree and a separate liberal arts degree. I should first admit that many things I am describing below were not entirely obvious to me when I was in the program. I do not blame myself—it was difficult to see the bigger picture when I was busy learning a new mathematical concept, preparing for a recital, and writing a paper on Kant's categorical imperative, all at the same time.

Looking back at my experience, ten years later, this program has allowed me to not only improve in my areas of focus but also grow as an intellectually curious individual. I have since formed the belief that the study of and exposure to different subjects allows us to explore our relationships with the past, present, and future, and it encourages us to ponder what it means to be alive. Music, math, psychology, philosophy—these are just different manifestations of the same quest to understand the meaning of us and the meaning of life. The liberal arts education made it clear that none of these subjects exist in silos. Instead, the confluence of thoughts, artistically or scientifically, theoretical or applied, allows us to define and interpret our very own existence. The Bard Conservatory education allows us to experience this confluence firsthand through the double degree requirement. Admittedly, while I have since had many moments of awakening, I have also come to the realization that there will always be many more questions left unanswered. My Bard experience is just the beginning of a lifelong journey to understanding myself in relation to the world.

Having become a college professor myself, my hope is to introduce to students the idea that, whatever subjects they choose to specialize in during their college years, these are ultimately just different ways of approaching and learning about life. I hope to share my college experience with students and provide them the gift of unceasing curiosity, just as what the Bard community has so generously given me.

Bihan Li '19, violin, went on from Bard to The Juilliard School. At Bard her second major was Asian Studies, with a senior thesis entitled Lin Yaoji: The Legend of Violin Education in China."

Starting with the first burst of fireworks, the sound of the band on the dance floor was gradually replaced by fireworks one after another. Like a carnival crowd, we were exhilarated by the countless sparks that filled the sky. Graduates with dreams, watching the waves of fireworks, with so many thoughts in their hearts, the longing forward for the journey to come, and backward for all that had happened here. Flashbacks of memory were like this night covered with fireworks, never enough.

Sitting in front of my computer, I pulled up the unforgettable graduation firework ceremony of a year ago. My thoughts were drawn back to the moment I first stepped onto this campus in 2014.

Bard is like the peach blossom spring in Tao Yuanming's poem. In this place seamlessly connected with nature, I have spent the most fantastic and challenging five years of my life. Here, everything is possible. Maybe before this, I was still a music high school student who was confused about the future, but Bard gave me the possibility of experiencing the unknown, allowing me to discover my potential in the exploration. I felt the charm of music in the piano room surrounded by "oil paintings", I was excited late into the night by an interesting math puzzle, I discussed the history of China's music education system in class with my professors, and I studied the light and shadow processing and the background music in favorite movies with my classmates. In this wonderland, I was not just a student who could only study music scores and thick music history books, but a girl who tried all kinds of impossible.

After five years, I finally understand that music does not only exist under the musician's fingers.

Everything I have experienced is more like a kind of self-cultivation, helping me better understand myself. Bard gave me the right to experience and to choose.

Now I choose to continue perfecting myself on the road of music. As a Juilliard graduate student in violin performance, I am full of confidence and have a sense of direction in my future. I have discussed the future planning with my friends more than once. Unfortunately, most of my music friends did not experience other things than music. They often feel lost because they have no chance to enrich their lives, and music seems to be no longer alive because of their monotonous lives. Bard helped me, as well as the other music students who chose the double-degree to explore our potential from multiple angles, and turn those countless sleepless nights of homework into our motivation. Bard made us strong and able to face the various challenges of life, no matter in which field. The double-degree program allowed me to view my life macroscopically, while assisting my career. I couldn't imagine being only a violinist; I would give presentations on the charts of supply and demand I made, I would stay in the library all afternoon to check the painting style of Kano school, and I would take a year to analyze the teaching system of the violin educator

I hope that Bard's double-degree concept can spread to more communities, so that music not only exists in the scores, but also integrates into the life of every musician, and lets the mind create music. This is the direction I will strive for in the future. I hope that as a teacher, I can help confused musicians find their way. I wish every musician to be no longer limited to the flow of notes, but to ride on the waves of thought.

Yang Li '11, violin, went on from Bard for her Masters' degree at The Juilliard School. She is currently associate concertmaster of the Dortmund Philharmonic Orchestra in Germany. Her second major at Bard was French Studies, and her senior project was entitled "An exploration of Ravel's opera *L'enfant et les sortilèges*".

Since graduating from Bard, I often come up with a question: what did I learn from my experience in this distinguished program?

Thinking about this very often reminded me of the meeting that was held for all the first-year students in the Conservatory. I asked a question, which sounded quite justified to me: "Which major would be most useful to the student?" With a confused look, the dean threw back more questions to me: "How do you define 'useful'? To help you find a job to earn a good amount of money? Do you not have any special interests or passions? Why must education be 'useful' in a utilitarian way?" At that time, these questions struck me so hard that I still remember them after all those years. Aren't we educated in order to learn something that will be of use to us in the future? If that's not the ultimate goal, then why should I waste my time and energy on learning? With these questions in mind, my busy college life started there—a place so beautiful as if being out of the world.

Although I had prepared myself, the difficulties I encountered were far beyond my expectation and preparation. Fortunately, people in the Bard Conservatory provided support and opened special courses to help us gradually move into the normal academic life. I remember that, when I was still a freshman, I usually stayed up after midnight to practice violin. We had to "squeeze" ourselves to complete the tasks we couldn't have imagined. However, we all did it at last, and it showed that the potential of human beings can always be further explored.

The class format at Bard was completely new to me; from my perspective, it should not be called a "class" because it was more like chatting. In some classes in the humanities, the students talked much more often than the professor did. If a student didn't speak up in the class throughout the entire semester, he/her might receive a lower grade. As time went by, and as I took more and more classes, I started to find a new source of energy. I heard many new ideas from other people and began to contemplate different questions myself. I still kept silent in class, but what others were discussing intrigued me. This kind of inspiration lasted even after the class was dismissed. I got to know many students equipped with active minds and original perspectives, who were able to enlighten their colleagues. Everyone wanted to be capable of doing that. Students were able to argue their side with clear evidence and reasoning. This is "critical thinking": an ability that Bard greatly values, encourages, and helps the students to learn.

Taking the "performance class" was one of the most memorable experiences. I had received music education of the highest standard since I was little, but what I had learned seemed to have no use to this class. There was another world: our fingers trained and skills practiced over the years seemed to be less worthy of talking than a beautiful but simple phrase created by the beginners. For my first performance in that class, I played a piece that I had brought to many auditions. I prepared it very well and was happy with it, hoping that I could "satisfy" Luis Garcia Renart, the professor. However, he didn't "grade" me after I finished playing; he rather encouraged me to play it again with a different feeling. "Have you ever thought of playing it *that* way? How many different ways can you imagine to play the same phrase?" We spent quite a while trying out different things, which made me confused. It seemed that I didn't manage to satisfy him? Otherwise, why would he come up with so many suggestions? Only after working with him did I realize that what he cared to do was to "open your mind." He wanted to remind you: don't forget what you need to *express* through your playing. He told me many times: "I don't want to listen to the violin; I want to listen to *you* playing the violin!" Before that, my goal was to play the piece well enough to pass the jury or audition, and I overlooked the fact that the best way to make music was to simply *express,* as those music lovers and amateurs would do. Taking this class, I started to realize why music education was not supposed to be "utilitarian": unlike fame, which comes from and spreads over the external world only, the satisfaction from the inside might be the long-term motivation and passion that intrigue you to keep going. These are the invaluable gains that I appreciate and will appreciate for the rest of my life.

In the end, I appreciate the fact that Bard led me out of the comparatively small world of music and introduced me to the outside space. Bard shaped me and made me become what I am, and I wish it will continue to guide me in the future to be a better person.

Zhi Ma '16, violin, went on to The Juilliard School, and then to a two-year training program in Shanghai, China and Hamburg, Germany. She is now a member of the Brandenburg State Opera Orchestra in Frankfurt an der Oder. Her second major at Bard was German Studies. with a senior project entitled "Exile on the Shorter End of Sun Avenue: An Analysis of Thomas Brussig's novel *Am kürzeren Ende der Sonnenallee.*"

The seminars at Bard were always fascinating, and of course nerve-wracking for me, when I still had trouble expressing my thoughts. I still feel so thankful for all the inspiring professors at Bard. I was always encouraged to think deeper and to talk more. Bard is where I first learned that there are lots of answers between yes and no, between black and white, and they may be the most intriguing ones. On any walk through Kline (the main dining hall), I would overhear people discussing what had happened in classes, what interesting arguments there had been. I was surprised to find people selecting classes because they want to learn and not because they need the credits. That was a major "cultural shock" for me as a Chinese kid, who never had the opportunity to select anything at school.

Everyone at Bard knows how lucky the Conservatory students are. I remember there was a mini movement called "occupy the Conservatory" initiated by the college music department students. (Of course that was a joke.)

We were privileged though. As Conservatory students, we had use of all the practice rooms on campus twentyfour-seven, and all classrooms whenever free; sometimes we could also sneak into the concert hall to run through our performance pieces; there were shuttle buses to the concert hall for people going to orchestra rehearsals, and on and on.

AND if you are lucky enough, which is quite often, you get to play chamber music with professors for the faculty-student chamber concert series! You will have the chance to experience how professors like Mr. Martin and Ms. Marka Gustavsson think of music during the process, while sitting next to you - everything is more direct and clear. So you see, as Conservatory students we were so spoiled.

How could I forget the lovely Eileen, who is a magical problem solver, a friend who listens to you whenever you need her. The most organized Fu-Chen, who has strict rules and an incredibly tender heart. And Luis, dear Luis, who seemed to know all the answers in music, the ones between black and white, yes and no. My violin teachers Mr. Jiang and Ms. Laurie Smukler, who helped me in so many ways that words can barely express how grateful I am to them. And lastly, Mr. Martin, who gave me the chance to have everything above, and who took care of us during the school year. During winter and summer breaks when we had trouble finding housing, he and Katherine let us stay in their house. The image of him with sparkling eyes announcing some new Conservatory projects is still so vivid to me.

Without Bard, the people I met and the time management struggles, I would not be the person I am today. Bard is a utopia. Bardians are urged to shape this utopia while themselves being shaped in the most nurturing way.

Jingyu Mao '19, clarinet, completed the M. Science degree (2020) in urban planning at the Lee Kuan Yew Center of Innovative Cities at the Singapore University of Technology and Design. His second major at Bard was Economics, with a senior project entitled, "The Road Ahead of Chinese SOEs".

When I first heard about the dual-degree program of Bard College Conservatory, I became very excited. The program seemed precisely designed to fill the "missing parts" of my education at the Music High School Affiliated with the Shanghai Conservatory of Music. At Bard, besides regular Conservatory courses, I could choose among courses in literature, science, the social studies and the humanities. These courses were like a gate for me, for exploring many areas of knowledge. In the First-Year Seminar I studied Plato, Lucretius, Montaigne, Rousseau, Marx, Weber, and Nietzsche, among others. In this course, I was a kind of philosophy traveler. In a Buddhism course, and in mathematics and chemistry, I learned things that I had never before thought I would learn. In the social science courses, I was led to the field of economics, which became my second major at Bard.

The experience of pursuing the two majors was exciting. For example, once when I was a third-year student, after I finished my Intermediate Microeconomics class at 11:50 am, I needed to rush to the Bito Concert Hall to play in a noon concert at 12:00 pm. I did not have any warm-up time before the concert, and needed to quickly put my clarinet together and go straight into the hall. I really enjoyed this crazy adventure. Another time, after I finished my Chamber Music class in the Conservatory at 1:30 pm, I needed to run to another side of the campus for my Finance class exam at 1:50 pm. I had only five minutes left for a quick last review before the exam, which forced me to squeeze all of my energy into the review. Such experiences trained me, physically and mentally, to adapt quickly to different environments. Also, I had to learn how to use limited time effectively. Most of all, I found that studying these two majors could even boost my motivation to study. When I felt mentally and physically tired from music practice, I found myself eager to study economics.

The same happened in the other direction: after long hours of studying economics, I was eager to return to music.

Besides the work in my two majors, I took great pleasure in extra-curricular activities, including the Bard College Investment Club (which I co-founded), the East Asian Food Club, the Zen Buddhism Club, the Ballet Club, the Bard Farm, and the Jewish Cultural Center. In the Bard Conservatory Orchestra, I had the opportunity to play overseas in the cities where so many great composers - Beethoven, Tchaikovsky, Shostakovich, Liszt, Chopin, Bartok, and Dvořák – spent most of their lives.

The experience of my double major studies at Bard created a spirit of joy in my academic life. I was proud that I was able to have a musician's life every day, and at the same time pursue the study of economics. Such a unique lifestyle enabled me to gradually become a multidisciplinary thinker. Bard provided me with an outstanding education to fulfill my thirst for knowledge of all kinds. The experience helped me explore comprehensively my personality, my personal interests, and the way of life that I seek.

After I graduated from Bard, I decided to explore the field of urban planning, and I was lucky to receive a full scholarship to pursue my Master's degree at the Lee Kuan Yew Center of Innovative Cities at the Singapore University of Technology and Design. This is my story over the past seven years. I started as a musician but finally became a student in urban planning. The transition looks quite extreme but actually was very natural. I have found that knowledge carries over from one field to the other, and that the networks I built in one area are networks that I can carry to the other area. Overall, "life that is diverse ......and a person who keeps doing a lot of things is really very important and that is the way that one should prepare oneself to deal with the world later.......young people should do many different things, and that will help prepare them to be creative" (Chan Heng Chee, from a lecture "Singapore and the World," presented in May, 2013 at the National University of Singapore).

Gitta Marko '19, violin, is pursuing graduate work in psychology at Edinburgh University. Her

second major at Bard was psychology, with a senior project entitled "An Exploration of Musical Performance Anxiety (MPA) and its Relation to Perfectionism and Performance."

This short piece is not about how I arrived at Bard clueless, nor is it about how, during the past five years, I have grown into a fully formed human that knows more about the world and the people around her than she ever thought was possible. Because yes, I do know much more about the world around me now, but perhaps even more importantly, I have learned that I am still clueless. Bard has taught me that this is an invaluable realization to have about oneself. Being (or at least feeling) clueless is an incredible asset, and I could not be more thankful for my undergraduate education for helping me come to terms with that.

Before you scoff, let me explain what I mean. From the first moment of *Language & Thinking*, I was encouraged to ask questions: questions that, until then, I thought were stupid, a waste of time, and just simply embarrassing to ask. I grew up within the Hungarian educational system, which, among its many strengths, unfortunately instilled in me a need to retreat and feel ashamed if I did not know something. Bard threw me in deep water the first day of class, during which I witnessed a professor jumping up and down inside an empty trash bag while reciting a poem. If that does not encourage one to ask questions, then I do not know what does!

What followed was two and a half weeks (but really, five years) of continuous and intense discomfort in a new reality – one in which I was forced to continually come to terms with the fact that there is an immense amount of information about the world I will never know. This discomfort has proven to be incredibly useful. As humans, our natural inclination is to move towards things that provide us pleasure and things that ease our pain and discomfort. One obvious way to do this is to ignore all unpleasant things in the world and exist in blissful ignorance. The other, and in some ways more challenging way to deal with discomfort is to keep exploring and keep asking questions. Some may argue that knowing more about the world will only lead to depression and existential dread, but in my personal experience, it has been quite the opposite. Knowing more about the world has made me aware of what I have yet to learn, and there is a certain kind of beauty in recognizing that.

The world will never be 'knowable', people will never be 'knowable', and even music will never be 'knowable'. This might seem frightening at first– what is the point of studying if I will never achieve a point at which I feel comfortable with the extent of my knowledge? That is exactly the point; for us, Bard Conservatory alumni, a continuous and never-ending exploration of the world around us is inevitable. We cannot ever *know*, so we explore.

This is a skill that we, as musicians, should always remember to practice. Of course, we can choose to settle for an obvious interpretation of a piece of music. We can also play a piece without considering the historical and political context within which it was created. And yes, we can definitely choose to only perform for the traditional classical music audience. Bard, however, has taught me that it is just as important (if not more important!) to play for audiences with limited access and exposure to classical music, like the people of Cuba, China or people who are incarcerated. By doing so, not only can we share our love of classical music with those who might be less familiar with it otherwise, but we can also inform our own musical decisions by expanding our worldview.

You can learn just as much from your audience as they can learn from you - this has been my mantra ever since I first experienced playing in a maximum-security prison. Once you start to internalize this thought, you can start to shed light on your own preconceptions about music and ingrained (perhaps bad) habits in your own practice. When you are asked questions (by those who are incarcerated, I might add) as poignant as, "How do you read music on a page? How can music, such an emotional thing, be notated?" or "What is the purpose of the conductor?

Does the orchestra really need one?", you are forced to reconsider the choices that you make in your everyday practice.

Experiences like these have had an invaluable effect on my own development both as a musician and a scholar. There is not one way to listen to music or play music, and Bard has taught me that all the different ways are equally important and beautiful. I could pretend to know all the answers to questions about classical music, but that would not only be an outrageous lie, but also take away the beauty of discovering, rediscovering, and realizing once again, that cluelessness is one of my biggest assets. The only way to develop as a human being and as a musician is by continually asking questions, and letting these questions stay just that - questions. We will never know all the answers anyway, so why not enjoy the ride?

Daniel Matei '19, percussion, went from Bard to the Contemporary Performance Program at the Manhattan School of Music in New York. At Bard his second major was Italian Studies, with a senior thesis entitled "Luigi Russolo: The Work and Influence of a Visionary – The Birth of Noise-Music."

It's been over a year since I graduated with a double degree from Bard, and the far-reaching impact of my studies upon my personal, musical and mental growth is more apparent with each passing day. Beyond the immense sense of accomplishment that comes with having completed a combined degree in music and liberal arts, I have become increasingly aware of the true extent to which those five years expanded my worldview, thought processes, and even the fundamental ways I think about music. My studies provided me with invaluable perspectives both practical and abstract. For example, the symbolic logic class I took during my freshman year taught me to form sound arguments, a skill which I apply daily in writing, speaking, and thinking. On the more abstract side, this class led to my awareness of the fascinating parallels between musical structures and language structures, introducing me to an interconnectedness of music and language that was previously unknown to me. As another example, my acoustics class taught me how to tune drums more effectively - which as a percussionist has obvious practical advantages - and also taught me that pitches are in fact very fast 'rhythms' (in that their identity, like rhythm, is contingent on frequency of sound, the beats just being too fast for the human ear to make out), a realization which still has lasting implications on how I conceive of music. In addition to the multifaceted benefits I gleaned from class material, the (sometimes daunting) challenge of juggling the conservatory classes with their academic counterparts was the best possible teacher of time management, and I am forever grateful for the supportive and nurturing environment that Bard provided me in which to harness this skill. I'm currently in the Contemporary Performance Program at Manhattan School of Music, and I feel that Bard prepared me to find my voice as a contemporary musician, while expanding my horizon in ways no other conservatory ever could.

Shawn Moore '11, violin, completed the MM in violin performance at the Yale School of Music in 2013. Since 2014 he has worked in China for Bard College in a variety of capacities, and performed throughout China. His second major at Bard was Asian Studies with a focus on Chinese language and literature. His senior project was entitled "In Search of Meaning: Three Short Stories of Modern Chinese Fiction in Translation."

The atmosphere of the early days of the Conservatory was that of a large, international family. Robert Martin, the founder and director, set this tone, and I think I can speak for many when I say that he felt like a grandfather to us all. I still fondly remember the tight-knit nature of the crew of friends from the first few cohorts. We bonded over music, academic challenges, and the exciting danger of being among the first to try a new project.

Studying at Bard opened up to me an entirely new world of possibility, and gave me opportunities I could not have dreamed of, growing up in the relatively staid suburb of Elgin, Illinois. I particularly enjoyed math and science subjects in high school, and when I first arrived at Bard, I briefly considered math or psychology as a major. By the second year, however, inspired and helped by many of my classmates from China, I began learning Mandarin and fell in love with it. This, for better or worse, changed the course of my life dramatically.

When I say Bard gave me opportunities, I mean that quite literally, because Bard offered me my first full-time job. In 2012, I joined the Bard Conservatory Orchestra tour for its China tour. I was asked to fill out the violin section and give the pre-concert lectures. One day, I was strolling through the atrium of the National Center for the Performing Arts in Beijing with Leon Botstein, Bard's long-time president, and he asked me whether I would like to move to China and work for Bard. I accepted immediately, and the direction of my life was forever altered.

I have spent the last 6 years in China working for Bard in a number of ways, including recruitment, partnership building, and alumni engagement. I founded and administered three partnerships for the Early College in China, and established our Beijing office. At the same time, I have continued to perform widely as a violinist, which has often offered a helpful complement to many of my directly Bard related obligations.

If I were given the opportunity to go back and change anything about my choices, I would certainly still go to Bard. Perhaps I would have focused a bit more on STEM, my only regret, but I would still have studied Mandarin, and I would still have come to China. Travelling and meeting students and educators across the country for these 6 years gave me an invaluable window through which to learn and understand more about China. Now more than ever, at a time of unprecedented stress for the US-China relationship, I think it is important that we maintain these connections.

Benjamin Pesetsky '11, composition, went from Bard to the "Logic Year" at the Institute for Logic, Language and Computation at the University of Amsterdam and then to graduate study at the Tufts University Music Department. He works now as a composer, program-note writer, and editor and consultant. His second major at Bard was philosophy, with a senior project entitled "The Philosophical Significance of Adequacy Results for Logical Systems."

Young musicians entering conservatory have far more experience and knowledge in their chosen field than most students starting higher education in other fields. They also tend to be unusually certain about what they want to be. An 18-year-old violinist, for example, probably already has the technical facility to play most of the repertoire, and intends to build a life around performing it. And a teenage composer—like I was—might already have an orchestra piece and a collection of chamber music in their portfolio, and hope their music will prove meaningful to the world. But it's easy to forget how unusual this is: most adults are not working professionally at something they have done since they were children, and most other occupations do not offer as strong a sense of purpose and identity as music. This is one of music's great attractions, but it also comes with the danger that you might be following a childhood talent or teenage obsession without really knowing who you are apart from it.

What Bard Conservatory's double-degree program offers, I think, is the opportunity to make a conscious choice to become an adult artist. To do so, you need to consider what else you might be, and seek other sources of meaning. For me, it was philosophy. Almost by chance, I took a course at Bard and found I had a knack for logic (the side of philosophy that overlaps into math), and then discovered I enjoyed the kinds of deep questioning and argumentation that philosophers engage in. After a stubbornly single-minded focus on music in high school, it was exhilarating to discover in college that I was good at something I hadn't previously known anything about. I wound my way through seminars on Aristotle, Kant, aesthetics, and even an upper-level math course, and graduated in 2011 with degrees in composition and philosophy.

There was never a precise moment I chose between the two, it was more of a protracted negotiation. I spent the following year at the University of Amsterdam, studying philosophical logic. I also took composition residencies at the Banff Center and other programs, which led to new connections, commissions, and collaborations. At some point, I realized that a career in philosophy was not for me, but I was also skeptical of the usual career path of 21st-century composers who pursue doctorates and aim for academic appointments. Perhaps it seems contradictory, but I think the depth of my undergraduate education, combined with my persistent independent streak, helped me imagine and commit to a different path.

For the last several years, I've made my way as a composer, program-note writer, and editor and consultant for prominent orchestras and concert series, including Boston's Handel and Haydn Society, the St. Louis Symphony, and the Tippet Rise Art Center. In this work, I continually draw on my liberal arts education. It's not easy to write or talk about music with insight and specificity, but bringing a philosopher's care with words and meaning to the task is a powerful skill. It's also something I've found sorely lacking in the profession at large. I once sat in a meeting where a prominent orchestra executive, without a hint of humor, compared classical music to selling different brands of frozen TV dinners. Mozart was "Lean Cuisine." Beethoven was "Mr. Hungry-Man." I have never felt farther removed from the intellectual environment of Bard, or wished more strongly to be back in Annandale.

It's a shocking example, but it represents the level of thought you sometimes find in the so-called music business. And it's exactly the kind of thing Bard Conservatory graduates are equipped to challenge. Many musicians—and even whole musical organizations—don't really understand what it is they're offering to society, what its human value is, or why they've chosen to do it. There's no one answer, of course, but to be an artist, you at least have to wonder at the question and be able to articulate a point of view. This doesn't mean learning more about music, it means learning more about yourself and more about the world.

Yiwen Shen '10, composition, completed his doctorate at the Juilliard School, and is now Assistant Dean of Performance Activities at the Tianjin Juilliard School in Tianjin, China. His second major at Bard was German Studies, and his senior project was entitled, "Gustav Mahler's Nirvana, A Study of *Das Lied von der Erde*."

I was lucky enough to be one of the first three composers to join the Bard Conservatory when it opened its composition program in 2006 and I graduated in 2010 with the inaugural class. As a composition major, I was offered invaluable experience. Not only did I study with world-class composers like Joan Tower and George Tsontakis, but I also had works performed frequently by ensembles such as the Da Capo Chamber Music Players and the Colorado Quartet. My violin concerto, *Mulan*, was premiered by the American Symphony Orchestra, led by Maestro Leon Botstein, at the commencement concert. Through these performance experiences I learned from the players what works and what does not work in my pieces. Even after my graduation, in 2012, I was honored to be commissioned and join the Bard Conservatory Orchestra on tour to China, during which my work, *The Sorrowful Song of Drunken Exaltation*, was premiered.

For my second major, I chose German Studies. I took the German Immersion course which met three hours a day, five days a week, for a semester and I continued studying 20 hours per week while living with German families during the summer. The German Studies department also supported my study in Berlin during the second summer. My senior project, "Gustav Mahler's Nirvana, A Study of *Das Lied von der Erde,*" traced the substantial literary changes passing from each poem's original Chinese, through French (another language I studied at Bard), to German and Bethge's paraphrase, to Mahler's final alteration. I discussed the complexities of Mahler's search, as a Jew, for a home in German music, literature, and philosophy. I tried to show how his achieving the final stage of stillness through Chinese poetry and Buddhism manifest themselves in the progress of *Das Lied von der Erde*, a journey from sorrowful earthly life to peaceful transcendental nirvana. My senior project later served as the foundation for my DMA dissertation at The Juilliard School: "Chinese Poetry Reimagined:The Musical Chinoiserie Movement In the Early-Twentieth-Century Austro-German Culture."

Bard not only taught me how to be a better musician, but, more importantly, it taught me how to think critically and become a well-rounded person, through its double-degree program and distribution requirements. It has been a little over 10 years since I graduated from Bard. Looking back, every step I made after graduation has benefited from what I learned and from the relationships I built while at Bard.

Yue Sun '12, violin, went on from Bard to the Juilliard School for her Master's degree. She is now a member of the Colorado Symphony Orchestra and of the DEKA String Quartet. Her second major at Bard was Psychology, and her senior project was entitled, "Do Urban Only Children in China Experience More Stress in Adulthood (than Adults with Siblings)? – Factors, Consequences ad Solutions.

In the first-year seminar in my freshmen year, I was required to read over 50 books on topics in science, literature, religion, philosophy and politics. It was difficult for me, considering my poor English and academic background, and it was also my first time "tasting" flavors of so many different topics. I felt the desire to know more. At that moment, I knew my "box" was unsealed.

Upon entering my sophomore year, I needed to choose my second major. I made a bold move by choosing psychology. I scored 40/100 in a psychology exam and it freaked out my mentor, who thought I might not be able to pass the course and graduate. I fell asleep in class because I could not understand the scientific terms and methods. Because of my poor academic background, I had to double or triple the time in order to understand the material. Many people thought I should re-consider my decision. But the "torture" from my first year had taught me one thing: I wanted and needed to step out of my comfort zone and do something different.

Then, many of my "firsts" occurred: the first time I stayed up the whole night to finish homework instead of practicing; the first time I played in five different chamber music groups in addition to giving two psychology presentations in one day; the first time I worked on a project with non-music majors; the first time I arrived 10 minutes early for an orchestra rehearsal; the first time I worked on a moderation paper for 12 hours non-stop, and then cried afterwards because I didn't pass; and lastly, the first time I finished my 100-pages senior project in psychology that even I thought it was impossible.

Then, almost simultaneously, I was accepted by Juilliard for the masters degree with full scholarship, which I also thought was impossible.

My life is different after all these, and the double-degree program has certainly played a big role in it. My life was like black and white before, but now I can see colors. The program broadened my view, and encouraged me to do more collaboration with others. Its diversity made me to think, and guided me to step out of my own "box". I am so fortunate and proud that I did the double-major in my best years. Many things I got from it are still helping me to make critical decisions to this day.

Andrés Martinez de Velasco '15, composition, worked after graduation at Bard College Berlin in

Admissions, and completed a Master's degree in physics at the Free University in Berlin. He is currently a PhD student in the Quantum Metrology and Laser Applications Research Group in the Physics Department of the Vrije Universiteit Amsterdam. His second major at Bard was physics, and his senior project was entitled "The Collective Cyclotron Motion of the Relativistic Plasma in Graphene."

What I most cherish about my Bard education, and what continues to define every new step of my life, is the fearless approach to artistic, scientific, and personal discovery that was instilled in me by my mentors. I took part in the conservatory's 5-year double-degree program as one of two composition students in my year, in a cohort of 12 musicians. I arrived with ambitions to become a great composer, the same ambitions I had had since I was kid! But, I also had to complete another degree, and even harder, I had to *choose* another degree. In an environment like Bard's, where a normal day could consist of a seminar on 20th century French poetry, followed by a composition lesson, an informal discussion of John Cage with fellow composers over lunch, a calculus lecture, and a midnight performance of Messiaen's *Quartet for the End of Time*, the only problem was that virtually everything was interesting. In my quest to settle on my second degree, I passed through literature, philosophy, and politics, only to end up in a program that no one who knew me could ever have predicted: physics. But, of course no one could have imagined it, because I had simply never had the chance (or shall I say *luck*) to study physics! How can we love something we've never met?!

In school, I was always a very strong student in humanities and social sciences, but a combination of uninspiring teachers and limited course offerings left the physical sciences as something I was decidedly uninterested in. All it took was a public lecture by one of Bard's physics professors and I was immediately hooked on a new world of ideas and concepts I had never encountered. Meanwhile, I continued my music studies and held strong to my life-long ambition to be a composer, supported by music teachers every bit as fascinating as those in physics. I was immersed in what now seems a dream world, where it was completely normal to have a rehearsal of my new string quartet, followed by a lecture on the quantum mechanics of the hydrogen atom. The fearlessness that I now cherish is exemplified precisely by the fact that this was a normal scenario, by the fact that we were not only encouraged, but expected to find our own, unique path.

Five years out of Bard, I have yet to find an environment as enriching as the one I had during my undergraduate years. I am now doing a PhD in atomic physics and continue to make my way as a composer, guided by the fearlessness at the center of my understanding of the Bard Conservatory's central philosophy: only by an unrestricted pursuit of our passions and ideas will we find our own voice as artists and thinkers, and our own path through life.

Yuan Xu '12, violin, received a Master of Science degree from the Columbia University Business School in 2015 and works now as Data Scientist at The Boston Consulting Group. His second major at Bard was Economics, and his senior thesis was entitled, "Optimal Pricing Strategy for New Electronic Goods."

After hours and hours of security check, passing through endless guards and white empty hallways, our orchestra finally arrived at the central hall of the NYSDOC Eastern Correctional Facility. For some inmates, this is the maximum-security prison where they would spend their entire life, and for some others, this was also the place where they would have their very first opportunity to hear classical orchestral music, live.

An orchestra performing deep inside the walls and barbwires of a prison? That did not sound right to me at first. Nevertheless, compared with many of our later concerts, such as the ones in Lincoln Center, National Center for the Performing Arts in Beijing, Hong Kong Cultural Center, Dr. Sun Yat-Sen's Memorial Hall in Taipei, and others, this was among the most memorable.

When our nearly 50-member orchestra squeezed onto the small stage, I sat so close to the edge of the stage that falling off was a real concern. There was almost no sound reverberation in the hall. Our audience, rather than the classy ladies and gentlemen you often find in Carnegie Hall, consisted instead of roughly 200 inmates in their polo-shirt or T-shirt uniforms. And yet, on that day I could feel every note of Dvorak's New World Symphony speaking directly into the audience members' hearts. Later during the Q&A session, an inmate asked where classical music can be heard outside the prison so he could tell his wife and kids to go and experience it. We were all moved. At that moment, I couldn't help but remember a Sibelius quote from the Bard Music

Festival pamphlet: "Music begins where the possibilities of language end."

What does it mean to be a musician in today's society? How should the next generation of world class musicians be educated? During my study at the Bard Conservatory, I often wondered about these questions, and I was puzzled about why Bard insisted on a second major, other than music. After all, taking on a second major occupies a fair amount of time that could otherwise be dedicated to practicing the next Paganini piece, or doubling down on some fancy techniques.

I eventually found my answer through numerous concerts with great musicians, and masterclasses with world renowned violinists. What stood out most during my interactions with them was never their impeccable technique, but their deep, profound understanding of music. It made me think that to make a craftsman in music, it takes practice, concerts, competitions, etc., but to produce a master musician, it takes all of that plus a scholarly study of the music itself. That is something hard to get unless you take a step back, look into other fields, and triangulate a piece of music against history, philosophy, architecture, and more.

Many of my fellow Bard Conservatory students went into majors such as Russian, German, or French, where they became bilingual, or trilingual for some. They read literature, history, and even spent a summer in those countries to really understand how a piece of music could weave into the very fabric of the society. In comparison, my second major choice could almost be considered "eccentric": economics and math. This is probably the most distant major from music, yet I still found symmetry between Bach's music and complex math theories. Both are logical, delicate, and full of structured beauty, as if they were born to be served together.

In the First Year Seminar, we read books such as Darwin's "On Natural Selection", Plato's "The Republic", "The Book of Genesis", and "Manifesto of the Communist Party" by Marx and Engels. Reading them prompted contemplation about religion, about goals and meanings, about human nature. All urged a deeper level of thinking, not only about music but also about life itself. It amuses me that in my freshmen year, the question "What is the meaning of my life" bothered me considerably. I still don't have a perfect answer today, but I am grateful that the First Year Seminar got me started on the journey.

It is a blessing that Bard offered not only solid performing arts training but also high-quality education for the second major. Completing a double degree program in five years is no easy task. It took a lot of work, but all that effort paid off by opening up new opportunities I never thought possible. After college, Economics and Math transitioned into my main career track, though I have not lost my love for music. When reflecting on my path, I am amazed by how music has become an indispensable part of my identity.

"We are our choices," Jean-Paul Sartre said. Among the many choices that shaped me, the music education at Bard Conservatory turned out to be pivotal. Now as I progress in life, I feel fortunate that my education has equipped me with the foundation for good decision making, the knowledge to solve problems, and the techniques to implement changes in the years to come. If there were other young students with a musician dream, I would not hesitate to recommend Bard as a place to first find their true selves in liberal arts education, then to find music mastery in their true selves.

Wei Zhou '10, piano, went on from Bard to graduate study at Stony Brook University, where she completed in DMA in 2018. She is now a member of the faculty of Nanfang College, Sun Yat-Sen University, in Guangzhou. Her second major at Bard was French Studies, and her senior project, a translation from French to English and an analysis, was entitled "The Splendid Life of Robert Casadesus."

I consider myself one of the luckiest to be among those in the very first class of the Bard Conservatory. Even though it has been fifteen years since the first time I set my foot on the beautiful Bard campus, I can still recall vividly the joy and excitement that I felt at the moment. I spent 11 years at Bard, six years as an undergraduate student and five years as a collaborative pianist.

Reflecting upon these years, I have benefited the most from two elements. The first one is its people— faculty, staff and the students. All the faculty members with whom I interacted have not only top-notch skill and knowledge in their fields, but also have a genuine heart. They truly care about the students and are willing to take the time to answer any questions that the students have. The Conservatory faculty members are all performing artists and it makes a big difference in teaching when the teachers are still active performers. Their technique, knowledge and understanding in music are constantly evolving, so the students are always being inspired by new ideas. The staff at Bard are some of the most wonderful people that I know. They are always there to give support to the students, whatever their regular responsibilities. We learn a lot from our peers. Bard students come from very different backgrounds and have different passions in life. They engage in very open discussions, in and out of classrooms. Interacting with my peers has certainly broadened my horizons and taught me to always remain curious.

The second great benefit for me at Bard was the rigorous training in writing and reading. The Language and Thinking workshop, the First Year Seminars, the Senior Project - all were painfully difficult for me. However, surviving these classes allowed me to excel in further studies. Thanks to the training, graduate school was not a struggle. Moreover, often enough we get the first impression about a person through his/her writing. Having good writing skills ensures a smooth start, whether it is for a school application, a job application, even for an apartment application!

Each day, I try to be, for my students, the kind of caring and inspiring teacher that I love.

Ye Zi '16, viola, went from Bard for graduate studies at the University of Montreal, (DMA 2021). Her second major at Bard was French Studies,

and her senior project was entitled, "The Chinese Labor Corps in France during WWI."

The main reason I chose to come to Bard was the requirement to study a second major, because I always wanted to learn something new. The French Studies major that I chose had about 20 students, so each student received a lot of attention from the professors. I still remember how I struggled with Intensive French in my sophomore year. Thanks to Professor Éric Trudel, who patiently answered my questions after almost every class. I managed to make progress. Of course, besides studying French, I had to plan the time for practicing viola and for other courses in the Conservatory. That was the most stressful time during my years at Bard. Fortunately, I survived that semester and successfully passed the final exams. This was a precious experience for me, learning how to use time efficiently and how to deal with pressure. That is the most important thing I learned at Bard.

At Bard I had multiple opportunities to take all kinds of fascinating courses. For example, in the Human Rights course I watched Shoah, the longest (9 hours) documentary film I had ever seen. I had so many thoughts and reflections watching all the interviews of the survivors, the witnesses and the perpetrators. In an International Relations course, I learned about the kind of era we were living in and we are going to be facing. Through this course, my understanding of the world was clearer and more real. The Acoustics course was very magical for me as a musician. I learned how sound is transmitted in the air and how it spreads in different environments. Professor Justus Rosenberg who survived World War II and helped many people escape, taught the "Ten Plays that Shook the World" course. Just listening his stories in class was already miraculous, not to mention his fluency in different languages and his distinctive insights into life. For the Symbolic Logic course taught by Professor Robert Martin, I learned the charm and preciseness of logic. In my senior project, I learned how to do research.

My viola mentor, Mr. Steven Tenenbom, taught me how to think and play more independently. He always encouraged me to face difficulties positively and to be the best I could be. In 2015, as winner of the Conservatory's concerto competition, I had the honor of performing the Bloch Viola Suite under the baton of visiting conductor JoAnn Falleta. In the spring semester of 2014, I studied as the first exchange student at the University of Montreal in Canada, where I gained the confidence to live and study in a francophone city.

I never thought that I would have the opportunity to be exposed to so many new things outside of the music field, and I never thought that I would continue to study French after my undergraduate studies. I think all of this is because of Bard. It has guided me to where I am now.

ABOUT THE AUTHOR

Robert Martin is emeritus professor of Music and Philosophy at Bard College (Annandale-on-Hudson, New York). At Bard since 1994, Martin was founding director of the Conservatory of Music (2005) and held other administrative positions including vice president for Academic Affairs. He was Artistic Co-director of the Bard Music Festival from 1994 to 2017.

Martin studied cello at the Curtis Institute of Music with Leonard Rose and Orlando Cole, liberal arts at Haverford College, and philosophy at Yale University (PhD 1965). He pursued a dual career in music and in philosophy, holding joint appointments at several universities and serving as cellist of the Sequoia String Quartet from 1975 to 1985. He was Assistant Dean of Humanities at UCLA before coming to Bard. and served from 1999 to 2004 as president of Chamber Music America. He is editor of and contributor to many books and articles on philosophy and music.

www.ingramcontent.com/pod-product-compliance
Lightning Source LLC
LaVergne TN
LVHW052027080426
835513LV00018B/2194